IMAGES
of Sport

THE SCARBOROUGH CRICKET FESTIVAL

Peter May of Surrey and Ted Lester of Yorkshire walking out to bat for Mr T.N. Pearce's XI at Scarborough during a Festival Match *v.* Pakistan in 1954.

IMAGES
of Sport

THE SCARBOROUGH CRICKET FESTIVAL

Compiled by
William A. Powell

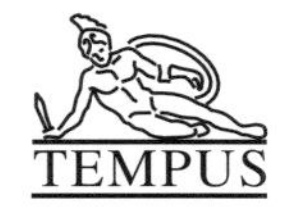

First published 1999

Tempus Publishing Limited
The Mill, Brimscombe Port,
Stroud, Gloucestershire, GL5 2QG

ISBN 0 7524 1638 3

Typesetting and origination by
Tempus Publishing Limited
Printed in Great Britain by
Midway Clark Printing, Wiltshire

This book is dedicated to Adam Robertson and Terence Sweeney who, coming from the North of England, would appreciate the camaraderie of the Scarborough Cricket Festival.

<u>Other cricket titles from Tempus Publishing:</u>

Glamorgan CCC
Glamorgan CCC*: the Second Selection*
Hampshire CCC
Leicestershire CCC
Somerset CCC
Surrey CCC
Worcestershire CCC
Yorkshire CCC

Contents

Foreword

When I was born, within the proverbial throw of a cricket ball from the North Marine Road, the Scarborough Festival had been in operation for almost fifty years. I first attended the Festival as a schoolboy when seven years of age – my parents always knew where I was at Festival times – but my real recollections stem from about 1934. At this time it was an integral part of the cricket calendar. It was the end of term celebrations for players and acquaintances to make new friends and to reminisce, a time of conviviality, banter and above all for Yorkshire hospitality and generosity at its best. This was a wondrous opportunity to absorb the atmosphere – the occasional cries of 'Rowntrees' pastilles, clear gums, sugared almonds' from sweet sellers plying their trade to the accompaniment of the Scarborough Town Silver Band which played continuously from lunch to close of play.

Play always began at noon with stumps being drawn at 6.00 p.m. Lunch was taken at 2.00 p.m. and tea on the field of play at 4.15 p.m. The opening match was always Yorkshire *v.* the MCC followed by either Mr H.D.G. Leveson-Gower's XI *v.* the MCC or the outgoing Tourists, North *v.* South or Gentlemen *v.* Players. The closing fixture was Mr H.D.G. Leveson-Gower's XI *v.* the Tourists, a splendid finale bringing together an array of quite unforgettable talent. The Festival itself closed with a rendition by the band of *Auld Lang Syne* followed by the National Anthem, both of which were traditionally observed.

On a strictly personal basis, my involvement stretches over sixty years. Initially I was a junior spectator and on one memorable occasion (1934) I was a ball retriever as Don Bradman scored an incredible 132 in 1½ hours off bowlers of the calibre of Farnes, Nichols, Bowes and Verity. I soon graduated in 1936 to scoreboard operative – my first paid employment – and in those formative years I became familiar with my schoolboy heroes which no doubt influenced a lifelong career in cricket.

To an avid autograph hunter the Festival was paradise and two cricketers will always be remembered: the West Indian Ben Sealey who replicated his signature on a rubber stamp, which was as likely to finish on a forehead as in a book, and the Indian batsman Mushtaq Ali who gave away ½d with his signature, thereby assuring his popularity.

About this time I remember running an errand for Herbert Sutcliffe and was rewarded with a banana, albeit overripe. Little did I think that in the first Festival after the war I would actually play alongside him. This was the first of my ten Festival appearances – marking my final appearance against Pakistan with the last of my 26 first-class centuries. In those ten years I was privileged to play with and against the best international players from all parts of the world.

Once my playing days were over, I assumed the role of resident scorer, an office which I held for more than twenty-five years and during which time I scored runs and took wickets for many skilled players. On retirement I reverted to casual spectating and it is with much sadness that I now see a Festival in progressive decline. From necessity, not choice, the old format has long since gone and because of the ongoing structural changes in the present-day game and the non-availability of many leading players, the Festival is virtually incapable of resurrection without serious revision.

Maybe this pictorial representation by William Powell will provide the necessary inspiration to enable a viable survival plan to be devised so that future generations may derive as much pleasure from their memories as I now enjoy.

Ted Lester
Scarborough, North Yorkshire
June 1999

Introduction

The Scarborough Festival began as a series of first-class matches between invited teams or teams made up of invited individuals. The Festival has taken place annually since 1876 at North Marine Road, usually in September. In recent years, with the introduction of limited-overs matches since the establishment of The Fenner Trophy, followed by the Asda Trophy and the Tesco Trophy, the majority of matches have been of the one-day variety.

The Festival, now in its 123rd year, has survived for such a long time perhaps because it has been seen as first-class cricketers being on vacation, rather than playing continuous county matches day in, day out. During the inter-war years, and for many years afterwards, Mr H.D.G. Leveson-Gower's XI *v.* Tourists was often regarded as the sixth Test match. In 1938 Don Bradman's Australians were defeated, as the opposition side included six current Test cricketers. The fixture with the Australians ceased after 1964 as the tourists refused to play in the Festival for commercial reasons and because tours had become more gruelling and involved more travel around the county circuit.

The first Festival took place in 1876. The teams present included Rangers CC, Yorkshire CCC, MCC and Scarborough CC. Since 1876 a number of private teams have been represented at the Festival, including Lord Londesborough's XI, Mr C.I. (Buns) Thornton's XI (since 1871), Mr H.D.G. Leveson-Gower's XI, Mr T.N. Pearce's XI, D.B. Close's XI, Michael Parkinson's XI, Sir Tim Rice's XI and the Heartaches XI.

Mr C.I. Thornton established the link between the Festival and the MCC in 1871 by recruiting players for his team from the MCC. Soon the annual Yorkshire *v.* MCC fixture became the cornerstone of the Festival programme and lasted until 1971 – some hundred seasons – until expulsion. In 1921 Mr C.I. Thornton was given the Freedom of the Borough of Scarborough and he joined a very select list of Freemen. 'Buns' Thornton was succeeded in the role of team organizer by 'Shrimp' Leveson-Gower who began his association with the Festival in 1899 and continued until 1950. He was also made a Freeman of Scarborough in 1930. Leveson-Gower's XI *v.* Tourists was the highlight of many Festivals. In 1951 Leveson-Gower's successor was Tom Pearce, a former captain of Essex who had been a rugby referee. Pearce stood down after thirty years in 1981 when the Festival lost only its third occupant of the post in over one hundred years.

Yorkshire CCC's association with the Festival dates back to 1833, although the county club was only established in 1863. Matches have been played at Scarborough regularly every season since 1891. Lord Hawke was instrumental in creating the relationship between Yorkshire and the Scarborough CC. He made his debut at Scarborough in the 1881 Festival and was a regular visitor to Scarborough until his death. He too was made a Freeman of the Borough of Scarborough.

The most eagerly awaited tourists to the Festival have been the Australians, who first visited the ground in 1878. Watched by a crowd of over 15,000, Don Bradman captained the 1948 side in his last first-class appearance in England, finishing with 153 out of the tourists' total of 489 for 9 declared. During the match Don Bradman was made an Honorary Life Member of Yorkshire CCC.

The Gentlemen *v.* Players match was a very popular fixture which was introduced in 1885 and continued until 1962, when the distinction between amateur and professional cricketers was ended. Some 38 matches were played at Scarborough with the Players winning 15 and the Gentlemen 4, while 19 were drawn.

One-day cricket was introduced to the first-class game in 1963 with the establishment of the Gillette Cup competition. On Sundays, prior to the introduction of the John Player League, matches were played by the Rothmans Cavaliers. The side was a Rest of the World XI including cricketers from the West Indies, South Africa, Pakistan, India, New Zealand and Australia. In 1966 the Festival programme included the following four matches: Mr T.N. Pearce's XI *v.* West Indies, England XI *v.* Rest of the World XI, MCC *v.* Yorkshire and a Yorkshire county championship fixture. Ten years later, in 1976, a Prudential Cup match was staged between England and the West Indies at Scarborough as part of the August Festival of matches.

In 1970 a sponsorship agreement was set up with Messrs J.H. Fenner & Co. Ltd of Hull and a 60-over knockout competition between four chosen counties was born. After a couple of seasons the Fenner Trophy became a great success, continuing until 1981. Since 1982 sponsorship has continued with Asda Stores Ltd, the Scarborough Building Society, Ward's Building Products, Joshua Tetley, McCain Foods (GB) Limited, Plaxtons and Tesco Stores Ltd.

The list of past presidents of the Scarborough CC includes HRH the Duke of Edinburgh (1961), His Grace the Duke of Norfolk (1963), HRH the Duchess of Kent (1976), Brian Sellers (1965), Herbert Sutcliffe (1968) and Sir Leonard Hutton (1975 and 1986). A Centenary Festival was staged in 1986 and since then the Festival has tended to attract smaller crowds. During the 1999 cricket season, the Scarborough CC will celebrate their 150th anniversary with a carnival of cricket. The centre-piece Cricket Festival will include Yorkshire County Championship matches with Northamptonshire and Kent and National League one-day matches with Kent and Leicestershire in mid-July and early September. Other matches will include a six-a-side competition, a period-costume match and a match between Sir Tim Rice's Heartaches XI *v.* the Scarborough club.

This introduction cannot be concluded without thanks to Ted Lester, the Scarborough-born Yorkshire CCC player and latterly (until his retirement) the county official scorer, for his foreword to this photographic history of the Scarborough Cricket Festival. As Official Scorer for Pakistan, the Sri Lankans and Surrey CCC between 1987 and 1988, I had the pleasure of scoring one Test match, two first-class matches and one limited-overs match with Ted Lester. Finally, thanks to the many who have assisted me with this work; all those who have made some contribution are included in the acknowledgements.

William A. Powell
Hemel Hempstead, Hertfordshire
June 1999

Acknowledgements

The author would like to thank the following, who have assisted in a variety of ways in the preparation of this book:

Ted Lester, Vic and Jill Lewis, the late Ronald Harries, Donald Carr OBE, Eric Russell, David Hart, Peter W.G. Powell, the late Bob Jones, Brian Croudy, Brian Heald, Sohail Malik, Mick Pope, Roger Heavens, Chris Hassell, Tony Woodhouse, the late Charles Steggell, Dora Hall-Newman, Lisa Pursehouse, Mark Newton, Yorkshire CCC and the Scarborough Library.

I acknowledge the following sources of illustrations: Walker's Studios, F. Stanley Cheer photographer, the Ted Lester Collection, the Harries family collection, the Vic Lewis collection and my own collection of picture postcards. Apologies are offered to anyone whose photographs have inadvertently been used without acknowledgement.

One

Yorkshire and the Counties

The Yorkshire side that faced the MCC in 1925. From left to right: R. Kilner, A. Dolphin, Lord Hawke, W. Rhodes, G.G. Macaulay, M. Leyland, E. Oldroyd, Major A.W. Lupton (*captain*), H. Sutcliffe, P. Holmes, A. Waddington, E. Robinson. The match was drawn at 6.00 p.m. on the third day, despite Herbert Sutcliffe scoring 171 and Roy Kilner 100 not out in a Yorkshire first innings total of 450 for 6 declared.

Major A.W. Lupton, captain of Yorkshire, and Wilfred Rhodes walking out to field for Yorkshire at Scarborough during a Festival match against the MCC in 1926.

Herbert Sutcliffe and Percy Holmes, both of Yorkshire, walking out to bat for their county at Scarborough during a Festival match against the MCC in 1926. The pair attended 133 for the first wicket with Herbert Sutcliffe scoring 72 and Percy Holmes 109 not out.

The Yorkshire side which played the MCC at the Festival in 1928. From left to right: E. Robinson, E. Oldroyd, G.G. Macaulay, W.A. Worsley (*captain*), A. Wood, M. Leyland, W. Rhodes, W. Barber, F. Dennis, H. Sutcliffe, P. Holmes. The MCC won on first innings by 79 runs. The match was drawn at 6.00 p.m. on the third day.

Arthur Mitchell and Wilfred Barber walking out to bat for Yorkshire at Scarborough during a Festival Match *v.* the MCC in 1929. The pair put on 74 for the first wicket, with Mitchell scoring 22 and Barber 51.

The Yorkshire side at their match against the MCC in 1929. From left to right: E. Robinson, F. Dennis, W. Rhodes, W.A. Worsley (*captain*), G.H. Hirst, F.E. Greenwood, M. Leyland, G.G. Macaulay, A. Mitchell, A. Wood, W. Barber. Yorkshire won by four wickets at 5.58 p.m. on the third day.

The Yorkshire side that faced the MCC in 1930. From left to right: H. Sutcliffe, W. Rhodes, E. Robinson, E. Oldroyd, P. Holmes, F. Dennis, A.T. Barber (*captain*), G.G. Macaulay, A. Wood, A. Mitchell, M. Leyland. The match was drawn.

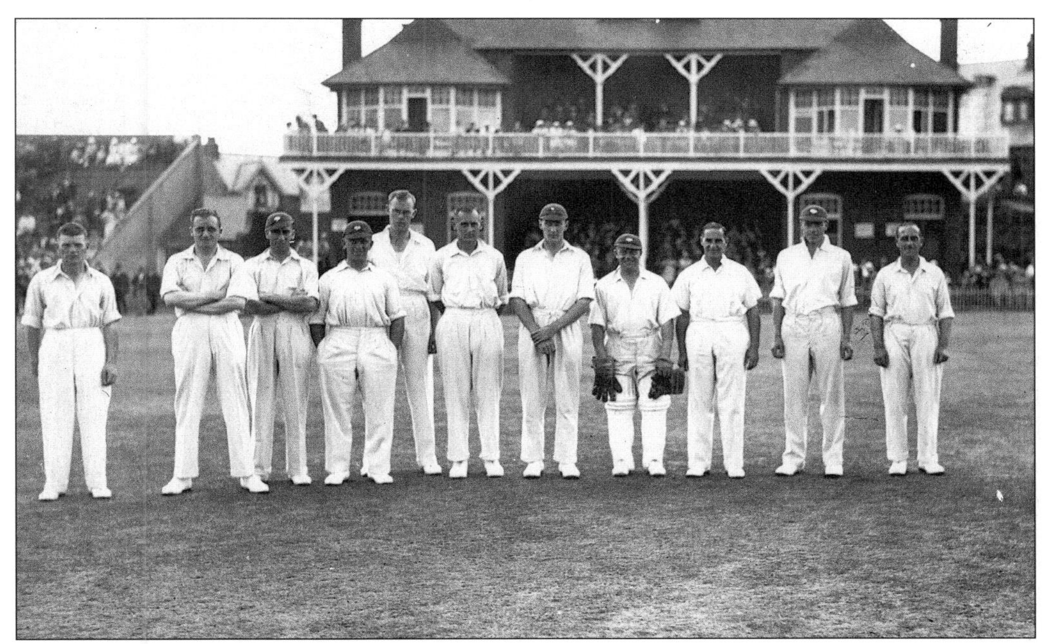

The Yorkshire side at Scarborough in 1930. From left to right: W. Barber, G.G. Macaulay, E. Robinson, M. Leyland, W.E. Bowes, H. Verity, A.T. Barber (*captain*), A. Wood, H. Sutcliffe, A. Mitchell, P. Holmes.

Yorkshire CCC at their match against the MCC in 1931. From left to right: A. Wood, W. Barber, M. Leyland, G.G. Macaulay, H. Verity, W.E. Bowes, F.E. Greenwood (*captain*), H. Sutcliffe, E. Robinson, E. Oldroyd, P. Holmes. The match was abandoned (because of rain) at 3.00 p.m. on the third day.

The Yorkshire side that played Essex in 1932. From left to right: F. Dennis, A. Wood, A.C. Rhodes, M. Leyland, A. Mitchell, H. Sutcliffe, H. Verity, A.B. Sellers, H. Fisher, W.E. Bowes. Yorkshire won by an innings and 8 runs at 2.18 p.m. on the third day and so achieved the double over Essex. Earlier in the season at Leyton, Percy Holmes (224 not out) and Herbert Sutcliffe (313 not out) had managed a first wicket world record partnership of 555 against Essex who were on that occasion soundly beaten by an innings and 313 runs.

Seen here at Scarborough for the county championship clash with Yorkshire in 1932 are the Essex players (from left to right) K. Farnes, J.R. Sheffield, J. O'Connor, M.S. Nichols, D.F. Pope, D.R. Wilcox, G.F. Eastman, R.M. Taylor, T.H. Wade, J.A. Cutmore, G.R. Brown. Yorkshire scored 476 for 9 declared, Essex replying with 325 and 143.

Brian Sellers, captain of Yorkshire, and Arthur Wood, wicketkeeper, walking out to bat for Yorkshire at Scarborough during a Festival match against the MCC in 1933.

Herbert Sutcliffe and Maurice Leyland, both of Yorkshire, walking out to bat for Yorkshire at Scarborough during a Festival match against the MCC in 1934. The pair added 49 for the fourth wicket, Herbert Sutcliffe scoring 74 and Maurice Leyland 42.

The Yorkshire side at the Festival in 1934. From left to right: A. Wood, W.E. Bowes, H. Verity, W. Barber, A. Mitchell, H. Sutcliffe, G.G. Macaulay, A. Waddington, M. Leyland, A.B. Sellers, E. Robinson.

Len Hutton and Wilfred Barber, both of Yorkshire, walking out to bat for Yorkshire at Scarborough during a Festival match against the MCC in 1935. The pair added 104 for the fourth wicket, Len Hutton scoring 92 and Wilfred Barber 60.

Herbert Sutcliffe and Len Hutton walking out to bat for Yorkshire at Scarborough during a Festival Match *v.* the MCC in 1937. The pair added 146 for the first wicket, Herbert Sutcliffe scoring 94 and Len Hutton 64 not out.

Wilfred Barber and Maurice Leyland of Yorkshire, preparing to face the MCC in 1937. The pair added 26 for the fourth wicket; Wilfred Barber scored 70 and Maurice Leyland 15.

The Yorkshire team which played the MCC at the 1937 Festival. From left to right: H. Verity, W.E. Bowes, N.W.D. Yardley, A.B. Sellers (*captain*), H. Sutcliffe, T.F. Smailes, W. Barber, A. Wood, M. Leyland, C. Turner, L. Hutton. Yorkshire won by eight wickets at 6.30 p.m. on the third day, largely thanks to Herbert Sutcliffe and Len Hutton, who scored 94 and 64 not out respectively.

Maurice Leyland and Arthur Wood, both of Yorkshire, prepare to bat for Yorkshire at Scarborough during a Festival match against the MCC in 1938. The pair added 62 for the seventh wicket, Maurice Leyland scoring 84 and Arthur Wood 45 not out.

Yorkshire CCC in 1947, when they played the MCC at the Festival. From left to right: J.H. Wardle, D.V. Brennan, W. Watson, E.P. Robinson, W.E. Bowes, A.B. Sellers (*captain*), N.W.D. Yardley, J.A. Richardson, L. Hutton, G.A. Smithson, W. Barber. The MCC won by 59 runs at 5.38 p.m. on the third day.

Len Hutton and Harry Halliday walking out to bat for Yorkshire at Scarborough during a Festival match against the MCC in 1948. Hutton scored 107 not out and Halliday 20, and the pair added 50 for the first wicket.

The Yorkshire side that faced the MCC in 1948. From left to right: A. Coxon, J.H. Wardle, D.V. Brennan, T.F. Smailes, N.W.D. Yardley (*captain*), A.B. Sellers, E.I. Lester, L. Hutton, H. Halliday J.V. Wilson, C.W. Foord. The match was drawn at 5.38 p.m. on the third day. The MCC scored 444 for 5 declared, with Martin Donnelly scoring 208 not out and Tom Pearce 134, and Yorkshire responded with 175 for 1, with Len Hutton scoring 107 not out.

Len Hutton and Frank Lowson, both of Yorkshire, walking out to bat for Yorkshire at Scarborough during a Festival match versus the MCC in 1949. The pair added 131 for the first wicket, Len Hutton scoring 147 and Frank Lowson 58.

The 1949 Yorkshire side which played the MCC. From left to right: G.A. Smithson, A. Coxon, D.V. Brennan, N.W.D. Yardley (*captain*), L. Hutton, E.P. Robinson, J.H. Wardle, E.I. Lester, J.V. Wilson, F.A. Lowson, D.B. Close. The MCC won by 1 run on first innings and the match was drawn at 6.00 p.m. on the third day. Three hundreds were recorded during the match: for Yorkshire by Len Hutton (147) and for the MCC by Denis Compton (127) and Ken Cranston (156 not out).

Yorkshire batsmen Harry Halliday and Norman Yardley walking out to face the MCC at Scarborough during a Festival match in 1952. The pair added 38 for the seventh wicket; Harry Halliday scored 50 and Norman Yardley 21.

Len Hutton and Frank Lowson walking out to bat for Yorkshire at Scarborough during a Festival match against the MCC in 1952. The pair added 86 for the first wicket, with Len Hutton scoring 103 and Frank Lowson 30.

The Yorkshire side that drew with the MCC at the 1952 Festival. From left to right: D.B. Close, E.P. Robinson, J.V. Wilson, E.I. Lester, J.H. Wardle, D.V. Brennan, N.W.D. Yardley (*captain*), F.A. Lowson, W. Watson, H. Halliday, L. Hutton. Yorkshire won by 29 runs on first innings but the match was drawn at 6.00 p.m. on the third day. Centuries were made by Frank Lowson (101) and Len Hutton (103 not out) for Yorkshire and for the MCC by Reg Simpson (101).

Len Hutton and Willie Watson walking out to bat for Yorkshire at Scarborough during a Festival match against the MCC in 1952.

Harry Halliday and Frank Lowson preparing to bat for Yorkshire at Scarborough during a Festival match versus the MCC in 1953. The pair added 160 for the first wicket. Frank Lowson scored 101 and Harry Halliday 87.

Brian Close and Willie Watson walking out to bat for Yorkshire against the MCC at Scarborough in 1954. Watson scored 34 not out and Close made 28; the pair added 42 for the fifth wicket.

Vic Wilson and Ray Illingworth about to bat for Yorkshire at Scarborough against the MCC in 1955. The pair added 128 for the fifth wicket, with Vic Wilson scoring 78 and Ray Illingworth 138.

Brian Close and Frank Lowson walking out to bat for Yorkshire at Scarborough during a Festival match versus the MCC in 1955. Close failed to score and Lowson made 11.

The Yorkshire side that met Worcestershire in 1957. From left to right: W.B. Stott, R. Illingworth, J.V. Wilson, R. Appleyard, W. Watson, W.H.H. Sutcliffe (*captain*), J.H. Wardle, J.G. Binks, D. Pickles, D.B. Close, F.S. Trueman. Yorkshire won by 25 runs on first innings but the match was drawn at 4.30 p.m. on the third day. Yorkshire made 291 in total, with Willie Watson scoring 102 and Brian Close 93. Worcestershire responded with 266, including 72 from Peter Richardson.

The Worcestershire side for the same match in 1957. From left to right: D.W. Richardson, R. Broadbent, G. Dews, L. Coldwell, M.J. Horton, R. Booth, J. Flavell, P.E. Richardson, D. Kenyon, G. Chesterton, L. Outschoorn.

Yorkshire at their match against the MCC in 1960. From left to right: D.B. Close, P.J. Sharpe, M.J. Cowan, W.B. Stott, J.V. Wilson (*captain*), R. Illingworth, D.E.V. Padgett, J.G. Binks, J.B. Bolus, D. Wilson, F.S. Trueman. The match was abandoned at 4.00 p.m. on the third day.

The Hampshire side (County Champions) before their match with Yorkshire (runners-up) in 1961. From left to right: D. Livingstone, D.W. White, L. Harrison, D. Shackleton, A.C.D. Ingleby-Mackenzie, R.E. Marshall, J.R. Gray, D.O. Baldry, P.J. Sainsbury, A.R. Wassell, H. Horton. Hampshire won by 71 runs on first innings and the match was drawn at 5.00 p.m. on the third day. Centuries were recorded for Hampshire by Henry Horton (160 not out) and Roy Marshall (104).

Scarborough Cricket Festival

President : Lt. Col. R. T. Stanyforth, C.V.O., M.C.

YORKSHIRE v. M.C.C.

Played on the Scarborough Cricket Ground August 31st, September 1st & 2nd, 1960

M.C.C.	First Innings		Second Innings	
1 J. H. Edrich............(Surrey)	lbw b Illingworth	41	b Illingworth	26
2 C. T. M. Pugh .... (Glos.)	c Cowan b Trueman...	4	b Trueman...............	4
3 K. F Barrington ......(Surrey)	b Cowan..................	16	b Illingworth	22
4 T. W. Graveney ......(Glos)	run out	12	c & b Wilson D.	6
5 D. R. W. Silk (Capt.) (S'mset)	c Trueman b Wilson D	13	b Illingworth	7
6 R. Swetman (w.k.)... (Surrey)	b Wilson D.	0	s Binks b Illingworth	14
7 A. S. Brown .... (Glos.)	c Close b Illingworth	17	c Close b Illingworth	53
8 G. W. Richardson ... (Derby)	c Sharpe b Wilson D	26	c sub b Illingworth...	0
9 D. A. Allen..............(Glos.)	not out	15	not out	1
10 D. R. Smith .... (Glos.)	lbw b Illingworth	0	b Trueman	0
11 H. J. Rhodes............(Derby)	not out	8	b Trueman	0
	b... lb 3 w... nb 1	4	b 3 lb... w... nb 1	4
	Total (9 wkts. dec.)	156	Total......	127

Fall of the Wickets

	1	2	3	4	5	6	7	8	9	10	1	2	3	4	5	6	7	8	9	10
	6	37	73	76	76	99	111	139	139	...	9	37	46	58	61	126	126	126	127	127

Analysis of Bowling	First Innings				Second Innings			
	Overs	Mdns.	Runs	Wkts	Overs	Mdns.	Runs	Wkts.
Trueman........................	7	2	14	1	8.4	1	27	3
Cowan	9	...	30	1	7	2	11	...
Illingworth	32	7	71	3	18	5	53	6
Wilson D.	21.3	9	37	3	19	5	32	1
	...	...	...	...	...	...	...	...
	...	...	...	...	...	...	...	...

YORKSHIRE	First Innings		Second Innings	
1 W. B. Stott........................	b Smith	5	....	...
2 J. B. Bolus	b Richardson	27	lbw b Rhodes	0
3 D. E. V. Padgett	b Smith	1	....	..
4 P. J. Sharpe........................	b Allen	45	not out	8
5 R. Illingworth	c Swetman b Smith ...	36	b Rhodes	0
6 D. B. Close	b Smith	8	....	...
7 J. V. Wilson (Capt.)............	c Barrington b Smith	33	not out	9
8 D. Wilson	c Barrington b Smith	8	....	...
9 F. S. Trueman	b Smith	9	....	...
10 J. G. Binks (w.k.)	not out	16	....	...
11 M. Cowan	....	..	....	...
	b 4 lb 2 w... nb 2	8	b... lb... w... nb 1	1
	Total (9 wkts. dec.)	196	Total......	18

Fall of the Wickets — Match Abandoned

	1	2	3	4	5	6	7	8	9	10	1	2	3	4	5	6	7	8	9	10
	10	16	62	97	128	139	157	171	196	...	1	1	...	...	...	...	...	...	...	...

Analysis of Bowling	First Innings				Second Innings			
	Overs	Mdns.	Runs	Wkts.	Overs	Mdns.	Runs	Wkts.
Rhodes	12	4	52	...	3	1	6	2
Smith	17.4	3	49	7	3	1	11	0
Richardson......................	8	1	29	1	...	...	...	...
Allen	21	6	58	1	...	...	...	...
Barrington	2	2	...	...	...	...	...	...
	...	...	...	...	...	...	...	...

Umpires : D. Davies & N. Oldfield — Scorer : C. Turner

Wickets pitched 11-30 a.m. Lunch 1-30 p.m. Tea 4-15 p.m. Stumps Drawn 6 p.m.

A New Ball may be taken, at the option of the fielding captain, after 75 overs or 200 runs

Wright & Co. Ltd., 15 North Street, Scarborough.

Fully printed scorecard for a match between Yorkshire and the MCC, 1960.

Tony Lewis of Cambridge University, Glamorgan and England seen at North Marine Road, Scarborough, during the Festival in 1961.

Two

Private Festival Teams

Mr C.I. Thornton's XI at Scarborough in 1925. From left to right, back row: G.E. Dennett (Gloucestershire), P. Holmes (Yorkshire), A.S. Kennedy (Hampshire), A.P.F. Chapman (Kent), A. Dolphin (Yorkshire), J.T. Tyldesley (Lancashire), G.O.B. Allen (Middlesex). Front row: J.C.W. McBryan (Somerset), E.H. Hendren (Middlesex), Mr C.I. Thornton, J.W.H.T. Douglas (Essex), W. Rhodes (Yorkshire).

Mr C.I. Thornton's XI the following year. From left to right: G.E. Dennett (Gloucestershire), A. Dolphin (Yorkshire), J.T. Tyldesley (Lancashire), P. Holmes (Yorkshire), J.C.W. McBryan (Somerset), G.O.B. Allen (Middlesex), A.S. Kennedy (Hampshire), J.W.H.T. Douglas (Essex), A.P.F. Chapman (Kent), E.H. Hendren (Middlesex), W. Rhodes (Yorkshire).

Mr C.I. Thornton's XI at a match against the Australians in 1926. From left to right: H. Strudwick (Surrey), J.T. Tyldesley (Lancashire), W. Rhodes (Yorkshire), G.T.S. Stevens (Middlesex), A.E.R. Gilligan (Sussex), Mr C.I. Thornton, V.W.C. Jupp (Northamptonshire), G.O.B. Allen (Middlesex), J.B. Hobbs (Surrey), H. Sutcliffe (Yorkshire), P. Holmes (Yorkshire), M.W. Tate (Sussex). The match was drawn at 5.00 p.m. on the third day. Mr Thornton's XI made 244 and 79 for 3, the Australians 194.

Lord Hawke's XI at their match *v.* the MCC (South African) XI in 1930. From left to right: K.S. Duleepsinhji (Sussex), G.O.B. Allen (Middlesex), A.T. Barber (Yorkshire), C.W.L. Parker (Gloucestershire), V.W.C. Jupp (Northamptonshire), F.W. Gilligan (Essex), W. Rhodes (Yorkshire), H. Sutcliffe (Yorkshire), A. Staples (Nottinghamshire), J.B. Hobbs (Surrey), P. Holmes (Yorkshire). The match was drawn and there was no play on the second day due to rain. Lord Hawke's XI made 345 for 9 declared, with the MCC South African XI responding with 341 for 4.

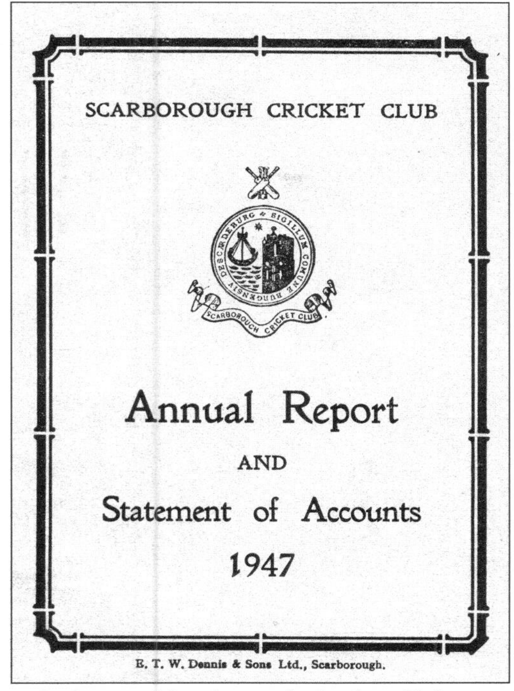

Left: Cover of Scarborough Cricket Club annual report and statement of accounts.
Right: Cover of the 1951 Scarborough Cricket Festival official souvenir programme No. 1.

Tom Pearce of Essex at Scarborough during the Cricket Festival in 1935. Born in Stoke Newington, London, in 1905, Tom Pearce was a very sound right-handed middle order batsman and right-arm medium-pace bowler. He played 231 matches for Essex between 1929 and 1950. He was captain of Essex from 1946 to 1949 and he toured abroad once with Martineau to Egypt in 1939. He scored 12,061 runs (av. 34.26) with a top score of 211 not out for Essex *v*. Leicestershire at Chalkwell Park, Westcliff-on-Sea, in 1948, took 15 wickets (av. 61.80) with a best of 4 for 12 and he held 153 catches. He selected his own team to play in the Scarborough Cricket Festival after he retired from the game. He was also a noted rugby football referee and officiated in many international matches.

Mr T.N. Pearce's XI in 1952 when they played India. From left to right: P.B.H. May (Surrey), A.V. Bedser (Surrey), C.N. McCarthy (South Africa), T.W. Graveney (Gloucestershire), R.T. Simpson (Nottinghamshire), L. Hutton (Yorkshire), T.G. Evans (Kent), T.E. Bailey (Essex), J.H. Wardle (Yorkshire), R. Smith (Essex), J.E. Walsh (Leicestershire). The Indians won by 190 runs on first innings. India made 258, including 72 from V.S. Hazare; Mr Pearce's XI scored 68 and 116 for 7.

Mr T.N. Pearce's XI *v.* Australia in 1953. From left to right: T.W. Graveney (Gloucestershire), A.V. Bedser (Surrey), P.B.H. May (Surrey), N.W.D. Yardley (Yorkshire), T.G. Evans (Kent), W.J. Edrich (Middlesex), T.E. Bailey (Essex), J.H. Wardle (Yorkshire), R. Tattersall (Lancashire), R.T. Simpson (Nottinghamshire), L. Hutton (Yorkshire). Australia won by two wickets at 5.58 p.m. on the third day. Mr T.N. Pearce's XI made 320 and 316 for 8 declared, with the Australians responding with 317 and 325 for 8.

Len Hutton of Yorkshire and Reg Simpson of Nottinghamshire walking out to bat for Mr T.N. Pearce's XI against the touring Australians in 1953. The pair added 71 for the first wicket, with Len Hutton scoring 49 and Reg Simpson 86.

Scarborough Cricket Festival

President : H.R.H. THE DUKE OF EDINBURGH, K.G.

T. N. PEARCE'S XI v. AUSTRALIA

Played on the Scarborough Cricket Ground on September 6th, 7th and 8th, 1961

T. N. PEARCE'S XI	First Innings		Second Innings	
1 J. H. Edrich............(Surrey)	st Jarman b Kline	110	c Benaud b Simpson...	20
2 G. J. Smith .... (Essex)	c Jarman b McKenzie...	8	st Jarman b Mackay ...	100
3 M. J. K. Smith ...(Warwick)	c McKenzie b Quick ...	2	c Booth b Mackay......	30
4 E. R. Dexter ....(Sussex)	c Simpson b Mackay...	57	b Mackay	110
5 P. B. H. May (Capt) (Surrey)	b Mackay	100	c & b Kline	41
6 J. M. Parks (WK) ...(Sussex)	c & b Benaud...........	2	c Booth b Mackay......	60
7 T. E. Bailey ....(Essex)	c O'Neill b Benaud ...	4	not out	7
8 D. A. Allen ....(Glos)	b Mackay	3	....	...
9 F. S. Trueman ....(Yorks)	not out	60	....	...
10 M. H. J. Allen ...(Northants)	not out	1	....	...
11 J. D. F. Larter ...(Northants)	....	...	....	...
	b 1 lb 7 w... nb...	8	b 4 lb 1 w... nb...	5
	Total (8 wkts. dec.)	375	Total (6 wkts. dec.)	373

Fall of the Wickets

1	2	3	4	5	6	7	8	9	10	1	2	3	4	5	6	7	8	9	10
13	99	105	202	209	235	262	359	...	...	40	188	235	295	347	373	...	...	...	...

Analysis of Bowling

	First Innings				Second Innings			
	Overs	Mdns.	Runs	Wkts.	Overs	Mdns.	Runs	Wkts.
Gaunt	6	...	23	...	8	2	12	...
McKenzie	5	3	7	1	9	2	35	...
Mackay	24	1	136	3	29	4	110	4
Quick	8	...	44	1	...	...	...	...
Kline	13	3	60	1	11	1	48	1
Benaud	13	1	59	2	...	...	...	...
Simpson	4	...	38	...	15	...	139	1
O'Neill	...	...	...	...	7	1	24	...

AUSTRALIA	First Innings		Second Innings	
1 R. Benaud (Capt)	c Parks b Trueman ...	1	c Parks b Dexter	41
2 R. B. Simpson	b Trueman..............	28	b Allen M	121
3 N. C. O'Neill	c Dexter b Allen D A	63	b Dexter	34
4 P. J. Burge	c Allen D b Allen M...	71	b Trueman..............	49
5 B. C. Booth	c Allen D b Trueman	77	b Trueman..............	38
6 K. Mackay	c Edrich b Allen D ...	33	c Allen D b Allen M...	14
7 G. D. McKenzie	b Trueman..............	1	not out	16
8 B. N. Jarman (w.k.)	not out	80	c Edrich b Allen D ...	32
9 I. W. Quick	b Bailey	17	not out	5
10 L. F. Kline	c Allen M b Bailey ...	16	....	...
11 R. A. Gaunt	b Allen M	2	....	...
	b 3 lb... w... nb...	3	b... lb 8 w 1 nb...	9
	Total......	392	Total......	359

Fall of the Wickets

1	2	3	4	5	6	7	8	9	10	1	2	3	4	5	6	7	8	9	10
3	68	143	165	238	312	314	360	378	392	100	177	213	283	292	318	348	...	...	...

Analysis of Bowling

	First Innings				Second Innings			
	Overs	Mdns.	Runs	Wkts.	Overs	Mdns.	Runs	Wkts.
Trueman......................	13	...	59	4	16	1	75	2
Larter	8	...	35	...	7	...	40	...
Bailey	12	2	50	2	4	...	32	...
Dexter	6	1	25	...	15	1	70	2
Allen M H J	17	3	102	2	16	2	80	2
Allen D A	15	2	118	2	12.1	...	53	1

Umpires : J. S. Buller, D. Davies. Scorers : H. L. Walker, J. Cameron

Wickets Pitched 11 a.m. Lunch 1-30 p.m. Tea 4-15 p.m. Stumps Drawn 5-30 p.m.

A New Ball may be taken at the option of the fielding Captain, after 85 overs or 200 runs

Wright & Co. Ltd., 15 North Street, Scarborough.

Fully printed scorecard for a match between T.N. Pearce's XI and Australia, 1961.

Tom Graveney of Gloucestershire and Denis Compton of Middlesex walking out to bat for Mr T.N. Pearce's XI at Scarborough during a Festival match against the touring South Africans in 1955. The pair shared a third-wicket partnership in the second innings of 63 runs, with Tom Graveney scoring 37 and Denis Compton 27.

Mr T.N. Pearce's XI *v.* Australia, 1956. From left to right: T.W. Graveney (Gloucestershire), T.G. Evans (Kent), T.E. Bailey (Essex), F.S. Trueman (Yorkshire), J.H. Wardle (Yorkshire), G. Goonesena (Nottinghamshire), P.W. Richardson (Worcestershire), W. Watson (Yorkshire), D.C.S. Compton (Middlesex), F.H. Tyson (Northamptonshire), D.J. Shepherd (Glamorgan). The Australians won by five wickets at 5.32 p.m. on the third day. Mr T.N. Pearce's XI made 272 for 9 and 200 for 7 both declared; the Australians made 280 for 7 declared and 193 for 5.

Peter Richardson of Worcestershire and Tom Graveney of Gloucestershire walking out to bat for Mr T.N. Pearce's XI in the same match. In the first innings Tom Graveney shared a first-wicket partnership of 25 with Peter Richardson and then went on to score 101 out of a total of 272 for 9 declared.

Mr T.N. Pearce's XI before they met the West Indies in 1957. From left to right: D.B. Close (Yorkshire), T.W. Graveney (Gloucestershire), F.H. Tyson (Northamptonshire), T.G. Evans (Kent), P.B.H. May (Surrey), P.W. Richardson (Worcestershire), T.E. Bailey (Essex), J.H. Wardle (Yorkshire), D.W. Richardson (Worcestershire), G.E. Tribe (Northamptonshire), F.S. Trueman (Yorkshire). Mr Pearce's XI won by 32 runs on first innings but the match was drawn at 6.00 p.m. on the third day. Mr T.N. Pearce's XI made 355 for 9 and 186 for 7 both declared; the West Indians replied with 323 for 7 declared and 151 for 8.

Jack Hobbs of Surrey and Herbert Sutcliffe of Yorkshire walking out to bat for Mr H.D.G. Leveson-Gower's XI at Scarborough during a Festival match versus the touring New Zealanders in 1931. The pair made a stand of 243 for the first wicket, with Jack Hobbs scoring 153 and Herbert Sutcliffe 126.

Mr H.D.G. Leveson-Gower's team before their match with the MCC Australian touring team in 1936. From left to right: A. Mitchell (Yorkshire), A.R. Gover (Surrey), M.S. Nichols (Essex), A. Wellard (Somerset), E.H. Hendren (Middlesex), A.B. Sellers (Yorkshire), F.R. Brown (Northamptonshire), D. Smith (Derbyshire), S.C. Griffith (Sussex), E. Robinson (Yorkshire), H. Sutcliffe (Yorkshire). The match was drawn at 6.00 p.m. on the third day. Centuries were scored for the MCC by Errol Holmes (146) and for Mr H.D.G. Leveson-Gower's XI by Herbert Sutcliffe (102).

Mr H.D.G. Leveson-Gower's XI *v.* All India, 1936. From left to right: M.S. Nichols (Essex), C.S. Dempster (Leicestershire), S.C. Griffith (Sussex), E.R.T. Holmes (Surrey), D. Smith (Derbyshire), A.R. Gover (Surrey), F.R. Brown (Northamptonshire), E.H. Hendren (Middlesex), A. Wellard (Somerset), C. Townsend (Derbyshire), H. Sutcliffe (Yorkshire). The match was drawn at 6.50 p.m. on the third day. The only hundred scored in the match was 140 by Mushtaq Ali for All India.

Eddie Paynter of Lancashire and Len Hutton of Yorkshire walking out to bat for Mr H.D.G. Leveson-Gower's XI at Scarborough during a Festival match against the Australians in 1937. The pair added 49 for the second wicket, Len Hutton scoring 88 and Eddie Paynter 30.

Mr H.D.G. Leveson-Gower's XI *v.* the MCC's Australian XI in 1937. Left to right: H. Verity (Yorkshire), E. Paynter (Lancashire), C.F. Walters (Worcestershire), J.M. Sims (Middlesex), G. Duckworth (Lancashire), G.O.B. Allen (Middlesex), J. Hardstaff (Nottinghamshire), R.E.S. Wyatt (Warwickshire), A. Townsend (Derbyshire), K. Farnes (Essex), M. Leyland (Yorkshire). The match was drawn at 6.00 p.m. on the third day.

Mr H.D.G. Leveson-Gower's XI when they played the Australians in 1938. From left to right: W.E. Bowes (Yorkshire), C.F. Walters (Worcestershire), H. Sutcliffe (Yorkshire), R.E.S. Wyatt (Warwickshire), P.A. Gibb (Essex), J. Hardstaff (Nottinghamshire), M. Leyland (Yorkshire), H. Verity (Yorkshire), K. Farnes (Essex), M.S. Nichols (Essex), L. Hutton (Yorkshire). Mr Leveson-Gower's XI won by ten wickets at 4.10 p.m. on the third day.

Martin Donnelly of New Zealand and Laurie Fishlock of Surrey walking out to bat for Mr H.D.G. Leveson-Gower's XI at Scarborough during a Festival match versus the Australians in 1948. The pair added 69 for the third wicket, Martin Donnelly scoring 36 and Laurie Fishlock 38.

Mr H.D.G. Leveson-Gower's XI *v*. the MCC South African XI in 1948. From left to right: E.H. Edrich (Lancashire), T.L. Pritchard (Warwickshire), J.C. Laker (Surrey), T.N. Pearce (Essex), M.P. Donnelly (Oxford University), W.W. Wooller (Glamorgan), R.E.S. Wyatt (Warwickshire), N.W.D. Yardley (Yorkshire), F.R. Brown (Northamptonshire), K. Cranston (Lancashire), J.G. Dewes (Middlesex). The MCC won by 74 runs on first innings and the match was drawn at 6.00 p.m. on the third day. Centuries were made for the MCC by Denis Compton (135 and 125 not out) and for Mr Leveson-Gower's XI by Freddie Brown (123).

Mr H.D.G. Leverson-Gower's XI before their meeting with the Australians in 1948. From left to right: T.G. Evans (Kent), T.L. Pritchard (Warwickshire), A.V. Bedser (Surrey), L. Hutton (Yorkshire), W.J. Edrich (Middlesex), M.P. Donnelly (Oxford University), N.W.D. Yardley (Yorkshire), R.W.V. Robins (Middlesex), F.R. Brown (Northamptonshire), J.C. Laker (Surrey), L.B. Fishlock (Surrey). The match was drawn at the end of the third day but the Australians won the first innings by 312 runs. The Australians finished on 489 for 8 declared with centuries by Sid Barnes (151) and Don Bradman (153 – his last hundred on English soil). Mr Leveson-Gower's XI made 177 and 75 for 2.

Mr H.D.G. Leverson-Gower's XI in 1960. From left to right: J.E. Walsh (Leicestershire), F.A. Lowson (Yorkshire), G. Lester (Leicestershire), E.I. Lester (Yorkshire), G.E. Tribe (Northamptonshire), W.H. Copson (Derbyshire), S.C. Griffith (Sussex), N.W.D. Yardley (Yorkshire), D.J. Insole (Essex), T.W. Graveney (Gloucestershire), T.L. Pritchard (Warwickshire).

Don Shepherd of Glamorgan and England at North Marine Road, Scarborough, during the Cricket Festival in 1961.

Three

Gents and Players

The Players XI, 1924. From left to right, back row: G.H. Hirst (Yorkshire), G.G. Macaulay (Yorkshire), J.T. Tyldesley (Lancashire), W.E. Astill (Leicestershire), J.W. Hearne (Middlesex), R. Kilner (Yorkshire), H. Sutcliffe (Yorkshire), Mr C.I. Thornton. Front row: E.H. Hendren (Middlesex), A.S. Kennedy (Hampshire), W. Rhodes (Yorkshire), P. Holmes (Yorkshire), W.W. Whysall (Nottinghamshire). The match was abandoned at 2.00 p.m. on the third day due to rain. The Players made 144 and 39 for 1, the Gentlemen 198.

The Players XI, 1925. From left to right: R. Kilner (Yorkshire), J.W. Hearne (Middlesex), A.S. Kennedy (Hampshire), W.W. Whysall (Nottinghamshire), E.H. Hendren (Middlesex), W.E. Astill (Leicestershire), P. Holmes (Yorkshire), G.G. Macaulay (Yorkshire), W. Rhodes (Yorkshire), J.T. Tyldesley (Lancashire), H. Sutcliffe (Yorkshire). The match was drawn at 6.00 p.m. on the third day.

Jack Hobbs of Surrey and William Whysall of Nottinghamshire walking out to bat for the Players at Scarborough during a Festival match against the Gentlemen in 1926. The pair added 54 for the first wicket with Jack Hobbs scoring 30 and William Whysall 71.

Johnny Douglas of Essex and Greville Stevens of Middlesex walking out to bat for the Gentlemen at Scarborough during a Festival match versus the Players in 1926.

The Gentlemen XI, 1926. From left to right: M. Falcon (Derbyshire), V.W.C. Jupp (Northamptonshire), K.S. Duleepsinjhi (Sussex), G. Challenor (West Indies), G.N. Crutchley (New Zealand), A.E.R. Gilligan (Sussex), N.E. Haig (Middlesex), J.W.H.T. Douglas (Essex), F.W. Gilligan (Essex), H.J. Enthoven (Cambridge University), G.T.S. Stevens (Middlesex). The match was drawn at 6.00 p.m. on the third day.

The Players XI for the same match in 1926. From left to right: H.A. Peach (Surrey), H. Strudwick (Surrey), J. Mercer (Glamorgan), J.A. Newman (Hampshire), G. Geary (Leicestershire), G.E. Tyldesley (Lancashire), J.B. Hobbs (Surrey), W.W. Whysall (Nottinghamshire), A.S. Kennedy (Hampshire), A. Sandham (Surrey), C.W.L. Parker (Gloucestershire).

Nigel Haig of Middlesex and Arthur Gilligan of Sussex walking out to bat for the Gentlemen at Scarborough during the 1926 Festival match against the Players.

Jack Hobbs of Surrey and Herbert Sutcliffe of Yorkshire walking out to bat for the Players at Scarborough during a Festival match against the Gentlemen in 1931. The pair added 227 for the first wicket with Jack Hobbs scoring 144 and Herbert Sutcliffe 96.

Herbert Sutcliffe of Yorkshire and Edward Dawson of Leicestershire walking out to bat for the Gentlemen at Scarborough during a Festival match against the Players in 1932.

The Gentlemen's XI, 1938. From left to right: P.A. Gibb (Essex), A.B. Sellers (Yorkshire), F.R. Brown (Northamptonshire), R.E.S. Wyatt (Warwickshire), D.R. Wilcox (Cambridge University),

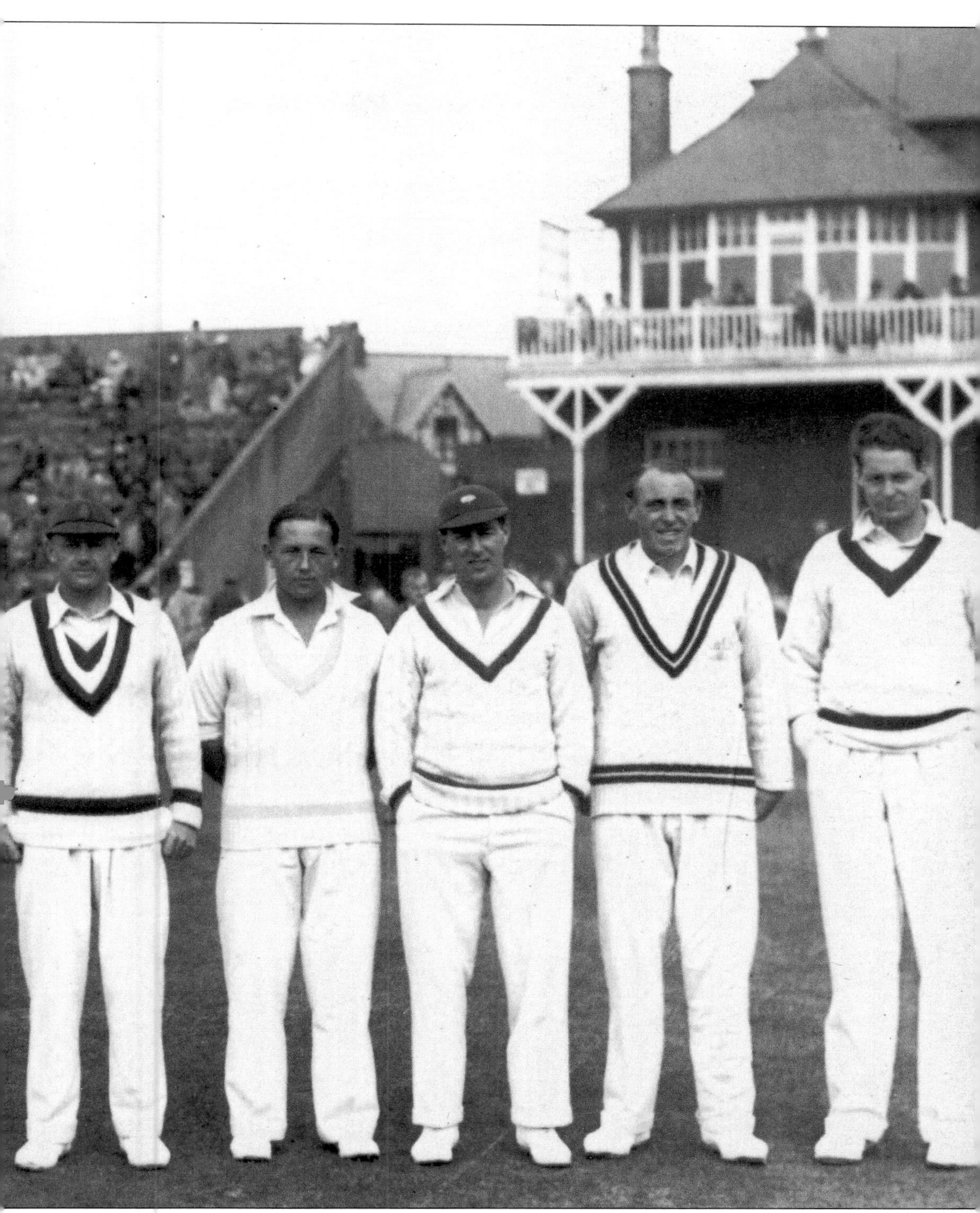

B.O. Allen (Cambridge University), G.O.B. Allen (Middlesex), S.C. Griffith (Cambridge University), N.W.D. Yardley (Yorkshire), H.M. Garland-Wells (Surrey), K. Farnes (Essex).

The Players' XI, 1938. From left to right: M.S. Nichols (Essex), L.B. Fishlock (Surrey), E.H. Hendren (Middlesex), W.E. Bowes (Yorkshire), A. Wellard (Somerset), H. Sutcliffe (Yorkshire), A. Wood (Yorkshire), A. Mitchell (Yorkshire), H. Verity (Yorkshire), C.J. Barnett (Gloucestershire), T.F. Smailes (Yorkshire).

The Gentlemen XI, 1947. From left to right: R.E.S. Wyatt (Warwickshire), J.L. Cheetham (Bridlington), W.J. Edrich (Middlesex), F.R. Brown (Northamptonshire), N.W.D. Yardley (Yorkshire), D.R. Wilcox (Essex), K. Cranston (Lancashire), A.W.H. Mallett (Essex), G.F.H. Heane (South Africa), W. Wooller (Glamorgan), M.P. Donnelly (Oxford University).

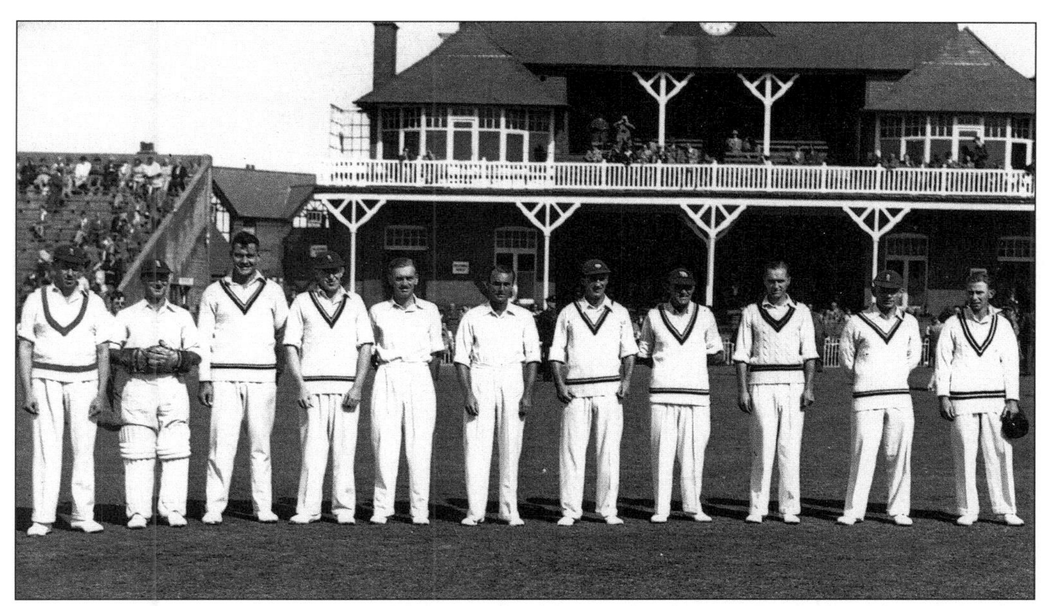

The Players XI, 1947. From left to right: R. Pollard (Lancashire), T.G. Evans (Kent), A.V. Bedser (Surrey), H.J. Butler (Nottinghamshire), R. Howorth (Worcestershire), J. Hardstaff (Nottinghamshire), L. Hutton (Yorkshire), L.B. Fishlock (Surrey), D. Brookes (Northamptonshire), C. Washbrook (Lancashire), D.G.W. Fletcher (Surrey).

Len Hutton of Yorkshire and Maurice Tompkin of Leicestershire walking out to bat for the Players at Scarborough during a Festival match against the Gentlemen in 1952. The pair added 156 for the fourth wicket; Maurice Tompkin scored 98 and Len Hutton 99.

Vic Wilson of Yorkshire and David Fletcher of Surrey preparing to bat for the Players at the same match. Vic Wilson scored 16 and David Fletcher 8.

The Gentlemen's team for the 1952 Festival match. From left to right: D.J. Insole (Essex), D.V. Brennan (Yorkshire), R.W.V. Robins (Middlesex), N.W.D. Yardley (Yorkshire), P.B.H. May (Surrey), R.T. Simpson (Nottinghamshire), T.E. Bailey (Essex), C.H. Palmer (Leicestershire), W.J. Edrich (Middlesex), C.N. McCarthy (South Africa), M.C. Cowdrey (Kent).

The Players team in 1952. From left to right: T.G. Evans (Kent), J.E. Walsh (Leicestershire), J.V. Wilson (Yorkshire), M. Tompkin (Leicestershire), E.A. Bedser (Surrey), L. Hutton (Yorkshire), T.W. Graveney (Gloucestershire), R. Smith (Essex), J.H. Wardle (Yorkshire), D.J. Shepherd (Glamorgan), D.G.W. Fletcher (Surrey).

Reg Simpson of Nottinghamshire and Doug Insole of Essex walking out to bat for the Gentlemen during the 1952 Players *v.* Gentlemen match. The pair added 35 for the first wicket, with Doug Insole scoring 21 and Reg Simpson 33.

Willie Watson of Yorkshire and Ray Smith of Essex walking out to bat for the Players at Scarborough during a Festival match against the Gentlemen in 1953. Willie Watson scored 143 not out and Ray Smith 32.

The Gentlemen XI for the same match. From left to right: D.V. Brennan (Yorkshire), T.E. Bailey (Essex), N.W.D. Yardley (Yorkshire), D.J. Insole (Essex), R.T. Simpson (Nottinghamshire), M.C. Cowdrey (Kent), W.J. Edrich (Middlesex), P.B.H. May (Surrey), W.H.H. Sutcliffe (Yorkshire), R.G. Marlar (Sussex), W.S. Surridge (Surrey).

The Players XI in 1953. From left to right: T.W. Graveney (Gloucestershire), T.G. Evans (Kent), L. Hutton (Yorkshire), J.H. Wardle (Yorkshire), M. Tompkin (Leicestershire), R. Tattersall (Lancashire), A.V. Bedser (Surrey), F.A. Lowson (Yorkshire), D.J. Shepherd (Glamorgan), R. Smith (Essex), W. Watson (Yorkshire).

Norman Yardley of Yorkshire and Trevor Bailey of Essex prepare to meet the Players at the 1955 Festival. The pair added 28 for the seventh wicket; Trevor Bailey scored 54 and Norman Yardley 7.

Vic Munden of Leicestershire and Fred Trueman of Yorkshire walking out to bat for the Players at Scarborough at the same 1955 match. The pair shared an eighth-wicket partnership of 12 runs; Vic Munden scored 61 and Fred Trueman 7.

The Gentlemen XI at the 1955 match. From left to right: G. Goonasena (Cambridge University), E.B. Lewis (Warwickshire), J.J. Warr (Middlesex), N.W.D. Yardley (Yorkshire), W.J. Edrich (Middlesex), P.E. Richardson (Worcestershire), T.E. Bailey (Kent), W.S. Surridge (Surrey), D.J. Insole (Essex), R.T. Simpson (Nottinghamshire), W.H.H. Sutcliffe (Yorkshire).

The 1955 Players team. From left to right: V.S. Munden (Leicestershire), G.O. Dawkes (Derbyshire), E.A. Bedser (Surrey), A.V. Bedser (Surrey), J.V. Wilson (Yorkshire), T.W. Graveney (Gloucestershire), R. Illingworth (Yorkshire), J.H. Wardle (Yorkshire), F.S. Trueman (Yorkshire), D.B. Close (Yorkshire), D.J. Shepherd (Glamorgan).

The Gentlemen XI in 1956. From left to right: T.E. Bailey (Essex), C.C.P. Williams (Oxford University), W.H.H. Sutcliffe (Yorkshire), J.J. Warr (Middlesex), A.C. Walton (Middlesex), W.J. Edrich (Middlesex), S. Singh (Cambridge University), J.F. Pretlove (Cambridge University), M.E.L. Melluish (Cambridge University), G. Goonesena (Nottinghamshire), D.J. Insole (Essex).

The Players team for the same year. From left to right: V.S. Munden (Leicestershire), F.H. Tyson (Northamptonshire), J.H. Wardle (Yorkshire), T.W. Graveney (Gloucestershire), D.C.S. Compton (Middlesex), A.E. Moss (Middlesex), W. Watson (Yorkshire), T.G. Evans (Kent), G. Barker (Essex), M.R. Hallam (Leicestershire), D.J. Shepherd (Glamorgan).

Bill Edrich of Middlesex and Billy Sutcliffe of Yorkshire walking out to bat for the Gentlemen at the 1956 Festival match. Bill Edrich scored 133 and 43 in the match and Billy Sutcliffe 4 and 23; they shared first-wicket partnerships of 10 and 58.

Players Tom Graveney of Gloucestershire and Willie Watson of Yorkshire meet the Gentlemen in the 1956 match. The pair added 150 for the third wicket, Tom Graveney scoring 124 and Willie Watson 72.

The Gentlemen XI in 1957. From left to right: E.R. Dexter (Sussex), P.E. Richardson (Worcestershire), M.J.K. Smith (Warwickshire), A.C. Walton (Oxford University), M.E.L. Melluish (Cambridge University), T.E. Bailey (Essex), J.J. Warr (Middlesex), D.J. Insole (Essex), W.J. Edrich (Middlesex), G. Goonesena (Nottinghamshire), W.H.H. Sutcliffe (Yorkshire).

The 1957 Players team. From left to right: D.W. Richardson (Worcestershire), B. Taylor (Essex), R.A. Gale (Middlesex), D.B. Close (Yorkshire), T.W. Graveney (Gloucestershire), T.G. Evans (Kent), J.H. Wardle (Yorkshire), F.S. Trueman (Yorkshire), F.H. Tyson (Northamptonshire), B.L. Reynolds (Northamptonshire), D.J. Shepherd (Glamorgan).

Brian 'Tonker' Taylor of Essex and Tom Graveney of Gloucestershire prepare to bat for the Players in the 1957 Festival match. The pair added 16 for the fourth wicket, with Tom Graveney scoring 13 and Brian Taylor 6.

Mike Smith of Warwickshire and Trevor Bailey of Essex go into bat for the Gentlemen at Scarborough during a Festival match against the Players in 1958. Mike Smith made 41 and Trevor Bailey 42.

The Gentlemen XI in 1958. From left to right: G. Goonesena (Cambridge University), E.R. Dexter (Sussex), E.C. Petrie (New Zealand), D.R.W. Silk (Somerset), M.J.K. Smith (Warwickshire), J.A. Bailey (Essex), T.E. Bailey (Essex), P.B.H. May (Surrey), J.J. Warr (Middlesex), P.E. Richardson (Worcestershire), D.J. Insole (Essex).

The Players in 1958. From left to right: D.W. Richardson (Worcestershire), R.A. Gale (Middlesex), P.J. Sainsbury (Hampshire), L. Morgan (Derbyshire), T.G. Evans (Kent), T.W. Graveney (Gloucestershire), J.V. Wilson (Yorkshire), B.L. Reynolds (Northamptonshire), J. Savage (Leicestershire), R.E. Marshall (Hampshire).

Mike Smith of Warwickshire and Ted Dexter of Sussex walking out to bat for the Gentlemen at the 1959 match against the Players. The pair added 26 for the third wicket; Ted Dexter scored 22 and Mike Smith 16.

The Gentlemen's team at the 1960 Festival. From left to right: J. Brown (Scotland), A. Hurd (Cambridge University), G.W. Richardson (Hampshire), J.J. Warr (Middlesex), D.J. Insole (Essex), T.E. Bailey (Essex), A.C.D. Ingleby-Mackenzie (Hampshire), E.R. Dexter (Sussex), D.R.W. Silk (Somerset), M.J.K. Smith (Warwickshire), C.T.M. Pugh (Gloucestershire).

Scarborough Cricket Festival

President : Lt. Col. R. T. Stanyforth, C.V.O., M.C.

GENTLEMEN v. PLAYERS

Played on the Scarborough Cricket Ground September 3rd, 5th & 6th, 1960

PLAYERS	First Innings		Second Innings	
1 R. E. Marshall.........(Hamps.)	b Richardson	32	c Insole b Warr	2
2 W. E. Russell ... (Middlesex)	lbw b Warr	27	b Warr	8
3 J. H. Edrich............(Surrey)	c Ing.-Mackenzie b Hurd	50	c Brown b Dexter ...	20
4 K. F Barrington ......(Surrey)	b Hurd	71	st Brown b Hurd	111
5 T. W. Graveney (Capt.)(Glos.)	run out	50	b Richardson	3
6 P. J. Sainsbury ...... (Hamps.)	b Bailey	21	c Dexter b Richardson	21
7 R. Swetman (w.k.)... (Surrey)	b Bailey	39	c Hurd b Dexter	14
8 B. R. Knight .... (Essex)	c Brown b Bailey	14	b Hurd	8
9 D. A. Allen...............(Glos.)	lbw b Bailey	1	c Ing-Mackenzie b Hurd	7
10 A. Moss .... (Middlesex)	not out	29	c Bailey b Hurd.........	1
11 H. J. Rhodes............(Derby)	not out	7	not out	17
	b 1 lb 7 w... nb 1	9	b 4 lb 2 w 1 nb 2	9
	Total (9 wkts. dec.)	350	Total......	221

Fall of the Wickets

1	2	3	4	5	6	7	8	9	10	1	2	3	4	5	6	7	8	9	10
49	61	153	191	251	262	288	292	335	...	3	23	31	86	92	154	191	196	198	221

Analysis of Bowling	First Innings				Second Innings			
	Overs	Mdns.	Runs	Wkts	Overs	Mdns.	Runs	Wkts.
Bailey	24	4	59	4	2	...	7	...
Warr	22	4	76	1	10	1	30	2
Dexter	12	3	17	...	14	1	43	2
Richardson.....................	11	...	40	1	8	2	19	2
Hurd	24	3	149	2	25	4	113	4
	...	...	...	...	...	...	...	..

GENTLEMEN	First Innings		Second Innings	
1 D. R. W. Silk ...... (Somerset)	b Sainsbury	119	c & b Allen	19
2 C. T. M Pugh .... (Glos.)	b Rhodes	15	b Rhodes	1
3 E. R. Dexter .... (Sussex)	c Graveney b Sainsbury	22	b Rhodes	56
4 M. J. K. Smith ...(Warwick)	c Russell b Sainsbury	63	c Moss b Sainsbury ...	74
5 T E. Bailey .... (Essex)	c Graveney b Russell	32	b Knight..................	10
6 D. J Insole (Capt.) ... (Essex)	b Allen	1	c Rhodes b Sainsbury	39
7 A.C.D.Ingleby-Mack'zie (H'ps)	b Rhodes	8	run out	17
8 G. W. Richardson ... (Derby)	b Moss....................	4	c Russell b Allen	22
9 J. Brown (w.k.) ... (Scotland)	b Rhodes..................	1	lbw b Sainsbury	1
10 J. J. Warr ...... (Middlesex)	st Swetman b Allen ...	16	b Allen	5
11 A Hurd .... (Essex)	not out	1	not out	1
	b 5 lb 2 w... nb 5	12	b 1 lb 3 w... nb 4	8
	Total......	294	Total......	253

Fall of the Wickets

1	2	3	4	5	6	7	8	9	10	1	2	3	4	5	6	7	8	9	10
19	53	175	229	230	247	258	261	290	294	8	49	125	147	202	208	244	245	249	253

Analysis of Bowling	First Innings				Second Innings			
	Overs	Mdns.	Runs	Wkts.	Overs	Mdns.	Runs	Wkts.
Rhodes	12	3	17	3	7	4	5	2
Moss	17	2	40	1	3	1	3	...
Knight.........................	8	2	27	...	5	1	15	1
Sainsbury	24	4	103	3	22	...	103	3
Allen	21	3	78	2	16.2	...	82	3
Barrington.....................	2	1	4	...	1	...	4	...
Russell	4	1	13	1	5	...	33	...

Umpires : N. Oldfield & H. G. Baldwin   Scorer : L. F. Franklin

Wickets pitched 11-30 a.m.   Lunch 1-30 p.m.   Tea 4-15 p.m.   Stumps Drawn 6 p.m.

A New Ball may be taken, at the option of the fielding captain, after 75 overs or 200 runs

Wright & Co. Ltd., 15 North Street, Scarborough.

Left: Donald Carr of Oxford University, Derbyshire and England at North Marine Road, Scarborough during the Cricket Festival in 1961.

Right: Fully printed scorecard for a match between the Gentlemen and Players, 1960.

The Gentlemen in 1961. From left to right: A.A. Baig (Oxford University), A.C. Smith (Warwickshire), J.M. Brearley (Cambridge University), R.M. Prideaux (Northamptonshire), D.B. Carr (Derbyshire), D. Kirby (Leicestershire), G.W. Richardson (Hampshire), T.E. Bailey (Essex), P.B.H. May (Surrey), O.S. Wheatley (Glamorgan), M.J.K. Smith (Warwickshire).

The Players XI in the same year. From left to right: B.S. Crump (Northamptonshire), M.H.J. Allen (Northamptonshire), B.R. Knight (Essex), J.H. Edrich (Surrey), N. Hill (Nottinghamshire), M.R. Hallam (Leicestershire), J. Milner (Essex), G. Millman (Nottinghamshire), J.D.F. Larter (Northamptonshire), J.S. Savage (Leicestershire), G.J. Smith (Essex).

Four

Tussles with the Tourists

The South African XI at their match against Mr C.I. Thornton's team in 1924. From left to right: J.M. Blankenberg, T.A. Ward, J.M.M. Commaille, H.W. Taylor, D.J. Meintjes, G.A.L. Hearne, S.J. Pegler, M.J. Susskind, C.P. Carter. A.D. Nourse and R.H. Catterall also played in the match but are not in the team group. Mr C.I. Thornton's XI won by an innings and 45 runs at 5.58 p.m. on the third day thanks to G.O.B. Allen's bowling – he took 10 for 118.

The West Indian team which faced Mr H.D.G. Leveson-Gower's XI in 1928. From left to right: C.R. Browne, F.R. Martin, E.L.G. Hoad, G. Francis, R.K. Nunes, L.N. Constantine, C.A. Roach, E.L. Bartlett, G. Challenor, J.A. Small, H.C. Griffith. Mr H.D.G. Leveson-Gower's XI won by 8 wickets, to which Jack Hobbs made a significant contribution with his 119 not out.

The South African XI in 1929. From left to right: J.A.J. Christy, H.G.O. Owen-Smith, A.J. Bell, Q. McMillan, E.L. Dalton, H.W. Taylor, C.L. Vincent, E.A. van der Merwe, I.J. Siedle, D.P.B. Morkel, B. Mitchell. Their match against Mr C.I. Thornton's XI was drawn at 6.00 p.m. on the third day.

The Australian team which played Mr H.D.G. Leveson-Gower's XI in 1930. From left to right: A. Kippax, W.A.S. Oldfield, C.V. Grimmett, S.J. McCabe, A.A. Jackson, T. Wall, A. Hurwood, V.Y. Richardson, P.M. Hornbrook, A.G. Fairfax, D.G. Bradman. The match was drawn.

Don Bradman of Australia takes to the field at North Marine Road during Australia's fixture with Mr H.D.G. Leveson-Gower's XI in 1930.

The South African wicketkeeper Horace Cameron takes the field at North Marine Road during the tourists' match with Mr H.D.G. Leveson-Gower's XI in 1935.

The New Zealand team which lost to Mr H.D.G. Leveson-Gower's XI in 1937. From left to right: T.C. Lowry, J.R. Lamason, A.W. Roberts, J. Cowie, D.A.R. Moloney, N.H. Gallichan, M.P. Donnelly, M.W. Wallace, W.A. Hadlee, J.L. Kerr, G.L. Weir. Mr H.D.G. Leveson-Gower's XI won by 145 runs at 4.26 p.m. on the third day.

Walter Hadlee and John Kerr walking out to bat for the touring New Zealanders at Scarborough during a Festival match versus Mr H.D.G. Leveson-Gower's XI in 1937. The pair added 60 for the first wicket, with Walter Hadlee scoring 55 and John Kerr 24.

Jack Fingleton and Bill Brown prepare to bat for Australia against Mr H.D.G. Leveson-Gower's XI in 1938. The pair added 36 for the first wicket.

The Australian team which faced Mr H.D.G. Leveson-Gower's XI in 1948. From left to right: S.G. Barnes, K.R. Miller, S.J.E. Loxton, D. Tallon, R.N. Harvey, I.W. Johnson, R.R. Lindwall, W.A. Johnston, D.G. Bradman, A.R. Morris, A.L. Hassett. This match was Don Bradman's last appearance in England. Australia won by 312 runs on first innings with Don Bradman scoring 153.

Arthur Morris and Sid Barnes walking out to bat for the touring Australians at Scarborough during the same Festival match. The pair added 102 for the first wicket; Sid Barnes scored 151 and Arthur Morris 62.

The New Zealand XI in 1949 at their fixture against Mr H.D.G. Leveson-Gower's XI. From left to right: G.O. Rabone, C.C. Burke, J.R. Reid, F.B. Smith, F.H.L. Mooney, W.A. Hadlee, M.W. Wallace, M.P. Donnelly, T.B. Burrt, H.B. Cave, B. Sutcliffe. New Zealand won by 6 wickets with Martin Donnelly scoring 145 in a first innings total of 338 all out.

Geoffrey Rabone and Bert Sutcliffe walking out to bat during the 1949 match against Mr H.D.G. Leveson-Gower's team. The pair added 5 for the first wicket, Bert Sutcliffe scoring 12 and Geoffrey Rabone 4.

Allan Rae and Jeffrey Stollmeyer prepare to bat for the touring West Indians at Scarborough during a Festival match versus Mr H.D.G. Leveson-Gower's XI in 1950. Allan Rae scored 51 and Jeffrey Stollmeyer 29.

South Africa's Cuan Macarthy pictured at North Marine Road during the Cricket Festival in 1951.

The Indian team that faced Mr T.N. Pearce's XI in 1952. From left to right: D.K. Gaekwad, P. Roy, R. Ghulam Ahmed, P.K. Sen, V.S. Hazare, P.R. Umrigar, D.G. Phadkar, G.S. Ramchand, H.G. Gaekwad, H.R. Adhikari, V.L. Manjrekar. India won on first innings by 190 runs but the match was drawn at 6.00 p.m. on the third day.

Pranab Roy and Dattajirao Gaekwad walking out to bat in the same match in 1952. The pair added 12 for the first wicket; Roy scored 51 and Gaekwad 8.

The Australians in 1953. From left to right: A.L. Hassett, A.R. Morris, A.K. Davidson, J. de Courcy, W.A. Johnston, J.C. Hill, G.B. Hole, G.R. Langley, R. Benaud, I.D. Craig, R.N. Harvey. The Australians beat Mr T.N. Pearce's XI by 2 wickets at 5.58 p.m. on the third day, when they reached 325 for 8, with Richie Benaud scoring 135 and Arthur Morris 70.

Arthur Morris and Graeme Hole preparing to bat in the same match against Mr T.N. Pearce's XI. The pair added 30 for the second wicket, Arthur Morris scoring 20 and Graeme Hole 52.

Lindsay Hassett and Alan Davidson both of Australia during the same Festival match in 1953. The pair added 84 for the seventh wicket; Lindsay Hassett scored 74 and Alan Davidson 39.

Captains Lindsay Hassett of Australia and Norman Yardley for Mr H.D.G. Leveson-Gower's XI take the field before the toss at North Marine Road in 1953.

The captains of the 1953 match at the toss.

The Pakistani XI in 1954 when they played Mr T.N. Pearce's team. From left to right: Shuja-ud-din, Hanif Mohammad, Khalid Wazir, Khan Mohammad, Imtiaz Ahmed, Maqsood Ahmed, Alim-ud-Din, Mahmood Hussain, Wazir Mohammad, Zulfiqar Ahmed, Waqar Hassan. Mr T.N. Pearce's XI won by nine wickets at 3.25 p.m. on the third day, thanks to Johnny Wardle's 6 for 67 and Alec Bedser's 3 for 70.

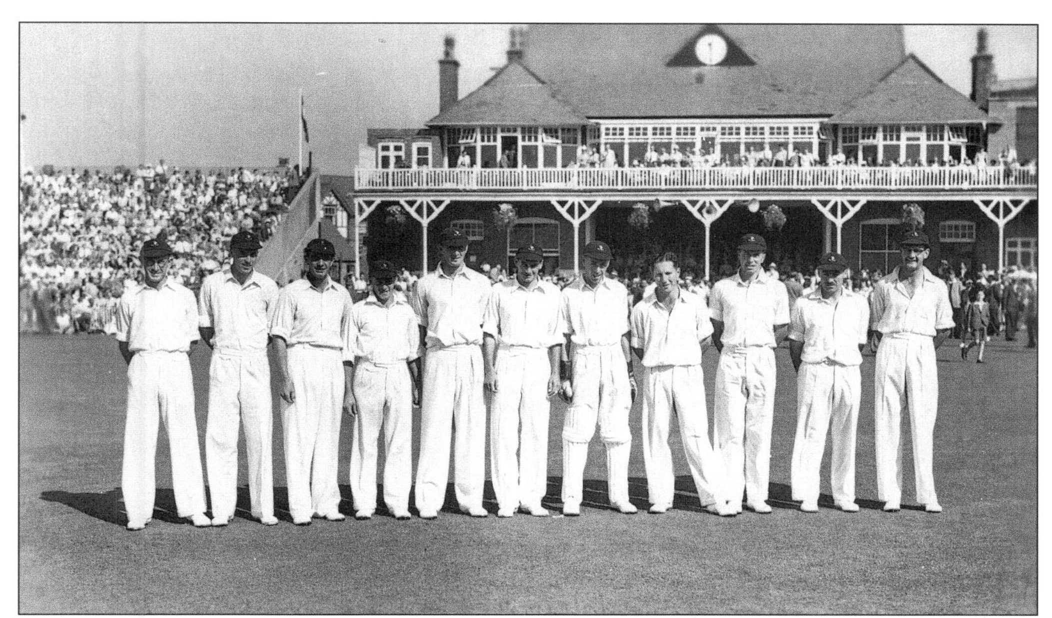

The 1955 South African tourists before their match against Mr T.N. Pearce's XI. From left to right: P.N.F. Mansell, T.L. Goddard, J.E. Cheetham, D.J. McGlew, P.S. Heine, H.J. Tayfield, J.H.B. Waite, R.A. McLean, A.R.A. Murray, W.R. Endean, P.L. Winslow. South Africa won by four wickets at 5.59 p.m. on the third day.

Trevor Goddard and Jackie McGlew, both of South Africa, walking out to bat against Mr T.N. Pearce's XI in 1955. The pair shared a first-wicket partnership of 105 in the second innings. Jackie McGlew scored 75 and Trevor Goddard 44 and the South Africans won the match by four wickets.

The 1956 Australian side that faced Mr T.N. Pearce's XI. From left to right: R.G. Archer, J.W. Rutherford, I.W. Johnson, K.R. Miller, K.D. MacKay, A.K. Davidson, L.V. Maddocks, R.N. Harvey, I.D. Craig, R. Benaud, J. Burke. The Australians won by five wickets at 5.32 p.m. on the third day, thanks to 78 from John Rutherford and 35 from Richie Benaud.

John Rutherford and Jim Burke walking out to bat for the touring Australians during the same match in 1956. The pair added 37 in the first innings and 68 in the second innings. Jim Burke was the top scorer with 94 and John Rutherford made 78.

The West Indians before their match versus Mr T.N. Pearce's XI in 1957. From left to right: A.G. Ganteaume, E.D. Weekes, R.B. Kanhai, A.L. Valentine, G.S. Sobers, C.L. Walcott, F.C.M. Alexander, N. Asgarali, O.G. Smith, D.T. Dewdney, R. Gilchrist. Mr T.N. Pearce's XI won on first innings by 32 runs thanks to 119 from Peter May. The match was drawn at 6.00 p.m. on the third day.

West Indians Andy Ganteaume and Nyron Asgarali take the field against Mr T.N. Pearce's XI in 1957. The pair shared first-wicket partnerships of 2 and 0 but in the first innings Andy Ganteaume went on to score 75 out of the West Indians' first innings total of 323 for 7 declared.

Nariman Contractor and Pranab Roy both of India about to bat for the touring Indians against Mr T.N. Pearce's XI in 1959. The pair added 27 for the first wicket in the first innings and 74 for the first wicket in the second innings.

The two minutes' silence for O.G. 'Collie' Smith, a popular member of the West Indies team, before a Festival match between India and Mr T.N. Pearce's XI in 1959. The Indian team (left) includes: P. Roy, N. Contractor, A.A. Baig, R.G. Nadkarni, C.G. Borde, D.K. Gaekwad, A.G. Kripal-Singh, J.M. Ghorpade, M.L. Jaismha, P.G. Joshi, Surendra Nath. Mr T.N. Pearce's XI includes: P.E. Richardson (Worcestershire), R.E. Marshall (Hampshire), M.J.K. Smith (Warwickshire), K.F. Barrington (Surrey), E.R. Dexter (Sussex), T.E. Bailey (Essex), R. Illingworth (Yorkshire), T.G. Evans (Kent), F.S. Trueman (Yorkshire), A.E. Moss (Middlesex), H.J. Rhodes (Derbyshire). Mr T.N. Pearce's XI won the match by five wickets at 5.25 p.m. on the third day, with a contribution of 62 not out from Ted Dexter.

The Pakistanis who played Mr T.N. Pearce's XI in 1962. From left to right: Shahid Mahmood, Nasim-ul-Ghani, Alim-ud-Din, Javed Burki, Imtiaz Ahmed, Fazal Mahmood, Intikhab Alam, Asif Ahmed, Antao D'Souza, Walis Mathias, Mushtaq Mohammad. The Pakistanis won by five wickets at 5.43 p.m. on the third day; Intikhab Alam scored 83 not out and Javed Burki 23 not out.

Fred Trueman of Yorkshire and jazz band-leader and avid cricket supporter Vic Lewis at Scarborough in 1955.

Australians Richie Benaud and Bob Simpson at a Festival match versus Mr T.N. Pearce's XI in 1961. The pair added exactly 100 for the first wicket in the second innings, with Bob Simpson scoring 121 and Richie Benaud 41.

Scarborough Cricket Club

President : The Right Hon. the EARL OF HALIFAX. D.L.

An England XI v. Sir Frank Worrell's West Indian XI

Played on the Scarborough Cricket Ground September 2nd, 3rd and 4th, 1964

	SIR FRANK WORRELL'S XI	First Innings		Second Innings	
1	R. E. Marshall	run out	32	b Knight	16
2	Cammie Smith	c Andrew b Knight	5	c Knight b Hobbs	13
3	S. Nurse	b Savage	116	c Knight b Hobbs	18
4	R. Kanhai	st Andrew b Savage	118	c Bailey b Savage	15
5	G. Sobers	not out	12	b Savage	44
6	B. F. Butcher	not out	16	c Knight b Savage	13
7	Sir Frank Worrell (Capt)		...	b Hobbs	1
8	D. Murray (wk)		..	b Savage	1
9	W. Hall			c Prideaux b Savage	9
10	L. King		...	not out	46
11	L. Gibbs		...	c Sub b Hobbs	10
		b 2 lb 6 w... nb...	8	b 8 lb 8 w... nb...	16
		Total (4 wkts. dec.)	307	Total......	202

Fall of the Wickets

1	2	3	4	5	6	7	8	9	10	1	2	3	4	5	6	7	8	9	10
17	55	264	281	...	...	...	...	...	...	29	29	65	65	66	103	106	136	151	202

Analysis of Bowling

	First Innings				Second Innings			
	Overs	Mdns.	Runs	Wkts.	Overs	Mdns.	Runs	Wkts.
White	13	1	44	0	3	0	14	0
Knight	18	3	57	1	6	0	15	1
Bailey	15	0	65	0	...	...	...	..
Hobbs	16	1	57	0	28.2	4	80	4
Savage	15	3	71	2	24	5	77	5
Milburn	1	0	5	0	...	...	...	...

	AN ENGLAND XI	First Innings		Second Innings	
1	J. B. Bolus (Notts)	c Hall b Sobers	90	not out	52
2	R. M. Prideaux (Northants)	c Marshall b Gibbs	51	c Nurse b Sobers	51
3	A. R. Lewis (Glamorgan)	c Murray b Sobers	2		
4	E. R. Dexter (Sussex)	not out	86	b King	21
5	C. Milburn (Northants)	c Marshall b Gibbs	16	b Gibbs	5
6	B. R. Knight (Essex)	not out	20		...
7	T. E. Bailey (Capt.) (Essex)		...		...
8	R. Hobbs (Essex)				...
9	K. V. Andrew (wk) (N'thnts)		...		...
10	D. W. White (Hants)		...		...
11	J. S. Savage (Leicester)		...		...
		b... lb 7 w... nb...	7	b 8 lb 3 w... nb...	11
		Total (4 wkts. dec.)	272	Total......	140

Fall of the Wickets

1	2	3	4	5	6	7	8	9	10	1	2	3	4	5	6	7	8	9	10
114	157	199	230	...	...	...	...	...	...	32	127	140	...	...	...	...	...	...	...

Analysis of Bowling

	First Innings				Second Innings			
	Overs	Mdns.	Runs	Wkts.	Overs	Mdns.	Runs	Wkts.
Hall	4	1	21	0	4	0	15	0
King	6	0	18	0	7	1	18	1
Sobers	27	1	134	2	14	3	47	1
Gibbs	24	8	92	2	10.5	0	49	1

Umpires : J. S. Buller, N. A. Oldfield   Scorer : E I. Lester

Wickets Pitched 11-30a.m.   Lunch 1-30 p.m.   Tea 4-15 p.m.   Stumps Drawn 6 p.m

A New Ball may be taken at the option of the fielding Captain, at 85 overs

Wright & Co., 15 North Street, Scarborough.

A fully completed scorecard from a match between an England XI and Sir Frank Worrell's West Indian XI in 1964.

Five

Famous Partners Take the Field

The MCC *v*. Australia, 1921. From left to right: G.G. Macauley (Yorkshire), M. Leyland (Yorkshire), F.C. Woolley (Kent), A.P.F. Chapman (Kent), W.R. Hammond (Gloucestershire), G. Duckworth (Lancashire), G.E. Tyldesley (Lancashire), H. Sutcliffe (Yorkshire), J.B. Hobbs (Surrey), E.H. Hendren (Middlesex), M.W. Tate (Sussex).

The MCC team that met Mr H.D.G. Leveson-Gower's XI at the Scarborough Festival of 1928. From left to right: H.J. Enthoven (Middlesex), A.E.R. Gilligan (Sussex), E.H. Hendren (Middlesex), F.W. Gilligan (Essex), V.W.C. Jupp (Northamptonshire),

H.D.G. Leveson-Gower (Surrey), J.W.H.T. Douglas (Essex), N.E. Haig (Middlesex), E.W. Dawson (Cambridge University), W.E. Astill (Leicestershire), F.J. Durston (Middlesex).

Patsy Hendren of Middlesex and Frank Gilligan of Essex walking out to bat for the MCC *v.* Yorkshire in 1934. The following year Gilligan emigrated to New Zealand and was Headmaster of Wanganui Grammar School for nineteen years.

Errol Holmes of Surrey and Frank Gilligan of Essex appearing for the MCC against Yorkshire in 1935. The pair added 67 for the ninth wicket; Errol Holmes scored 80 and Frank Gilligan 18 not out.

William 'Hopper' Levett of Kent and Denys Wilcox of Essex walking out to bat for the MCC at Scarborough during a Festival match against Yorkshire in 1937. The pair added 21 for the first wicket; Denys Wilcox scored 21 and 'Hopper' Levett 6.

Denys Wilcox of Essex and Bob Wyatt of Warwickshire appearing for the MCC *v*. Yorkshire in 1937. Denys Wilcox made 58 and Bob Wyatt 152 not out.

The MCC side that faced Yorkshire in 1938. From left to right: T.N. Pearce (Essex), J.M. Sims (Middlesex), C.I.J. Smith (Middlesex), W.J. Edrich (Middlesex), S.C. Griffith (Sussex), F.R. Brown (Northamptonshire), H.M. Garland-Wells (Surrey), G.O.B. Allen (Middlesex), D.R. Wilcox (Essex), R.E.S. Wyatt (Warwickshire), K. Farnes (Essex). The match was drawn at 6.00 p.m. on the third day.

Richard Howorth of Worcestershire and Syd Brown of Middlesex face Yorkshire for the MCC in 1947 The pair added 10 for the second wicket in both innings. Richard Howorth went on to score 61 in the first innings and Syd Brown 56 in the second innings.

The MCC beat Yorkshire at the 1947 Festival. The victorious team was comprised of, from left to right: G.F.H. Heane (South Africa), T.G. Evans (Kent), K. Cranston (Lancashire), J.A. Young (Middlesex), D.R. Wilcox (Essex), R.E.S. Wyatt (Warwickshire), R. Howorth (Worcestershire), A.W.H. Mallett (Essex), S.M. Brown (Middlesex), M.P. Donnelly (Oxford University), R. Pollard (Lancashire). The MCC won by 59 runs at 5.38 p.m. on the third day, with 362 and 159. Yorkshire responded with 257 and 205.

Martin Donnelly of New Zealand and Tom Pearce of Essex walking out to bat for the MCC *v.* Yorkshire in 1948. The pair made a successful partnership of 278 runs for the third wicket. Tom Pearce made 134 and Martin Donnelly 208 not out.

Freddie Brown of Northamptonshire and Bob Wyatt of Warwickshire appearing for the MCC *v*. Yorkshire in 1948.

The MCC Festival team in 1948. From left to right: T.G. Evans (Kent), T.N. Pearce (Essex), J.A. Young (Middlesex), G.F.H. Heane (South Africa), F.R. Brown (Northamptonshire), R.E.S. Wyatt (Warwickshire), W.W. Wooller (Glamorgan), K. Cranston (Lancashire), R. Pollard (Lancashire), J.G. Dewes (Middlesex), M.P. Donnelly (Oxford University).

Another MCC team in 1948. From left to right: R. Pollard (Lancashire), T.G. Evans (Kent), L. Hutton (Yorkshire), R.T. Simpson (Nottinghamshire), F.G. Mann (Middlesex), C.H. Palmer (Worcestershire), G.M. Emmett (Gloucestershire), W.H. Copson (Derbyshire), A.V. Bedser (Surrey), D.C.S. Compton (Middlesex), J.A. Young (Middlesex).

Syd Brown of Middlesex and Freddie Brown of Northamptonshire prepare to bat for the MCC at Scarborough against Yorkshire, in 1949. The pair added 47 for the second wicket; Freddie Brown scored 6 and Syd Brown 24.

The MCC *v*. Yorkshire, 1949. From left to right: G.O. Dawkes (Derbyshire), J.A. Young (Middlesex), F.G. Mann (Middlesex), F.R. Brown (Northamptonshire), R.E.S. Wyatt (Worcestershire), W.J. Edrich (Middlesex), T.N. Pearce (Essex), K. Cranston (Lancashire), V. Broderick (Northamptonshire), S.M. Brown (Middlesex), D.C.S. Compton (Middlesex). The MCC won on first innings by a single run and the match drawn at 6.00 p.m. on the third day. Yorkshire made 429 for 8 and 212 for 3 (both declared) and the MCC 430 for 9 declared and 109 for 5.

Bill Edrich of Middlesex and Doug Insole of Essex walking out to bat for the MCC *v*. Yorkshire in 1950. Bill Edrich scored 135 and Doug Insole 25 and between them added 72 for the fourth wicket.

Reg Simpson of Nottinghamshire and Michael Walford of Somerset prepare to meet Yorkshire for the MCC in 1950. The pair added 13 for the first wicket; Reg Simpson scored 28 and Michael Walford 4.

Bill Edrich of Middlesex and Colin Cowdrey of Kent walking out to bat for the MCC *v*. Yorkshire in 1953. They added 61 for the third wicket with Bill Edrich scoring 47 and Colin Cowdrey 33.

The MCC side that drew with Yorkshire in 1953. From left to right: T.W. Graveney (Gloucestershire), D.J. Insole (Essex), T.G. Evans (Kent), J.J. Warr (Middlesex), T.E. Bailey (Essex), W.J. Edrich (Middlesex), M.C. Cowdrey (Kent), F.J. Titmus (Middlesex), R.T. Simpson (Nottinghamshire), D.J. Shepherd (Glamorgan), W.H.H. Sutcliffe (Yorkshire). Yorkshire took the first innings by 29 runs.

Billy Sutcliffe of Yorkshire and Bill Edrich of Middlesex walking out to bat for the MCC against Yorkshire in 1954. The pair added 54 for the third wicket, with Billy Sutcliffe scoring 54 and Bill Edrich 34.

Tom Graveney of Gloucestershire and Don Shepherd of Glamorgan appear for the MCC *v.* Yorkshire in 1955. Their scores of 40 not out and 5, respectively, contributed to an eighth-wicket partnership of 8 runs.

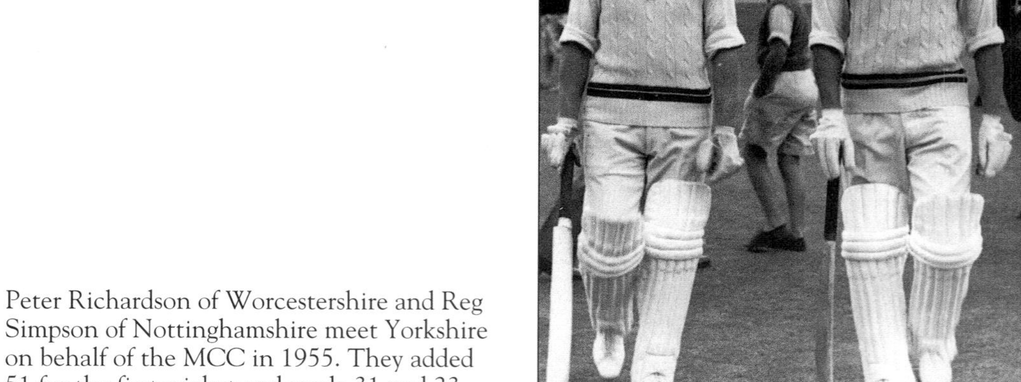

Peter Richardson of Worcestershire and Reg Simpson of Nottinghamshire meet Yorkshire on behalf of the MCC in 1955. They added 51 for the first wicket and made 31 and 23 respectively.

The MCC *v.* Yorkshire in 1955. From left to right: P.A. Gibb (Essex), V.S. Munden (Leicestershire), B.D. Wells (Gloucestershire), D.J. Shepherd (Glamorgan), W.H.H. Sutcliffe (Yorkshire), T.E. Bailey (Essex), D.J. Insole (Essex), T.W. Graveney (Gloucestershire), T.A. Hall (Somerset), R.T. Simpson (Nottinghamshire), P.W. Richardson (Worcestershire). Yorkshire won by 152 runs on the first innings but the match was drawn at 6.00 p.m. on the third day.

The MCC *v.* Yorkshire in 1956. From left to right: F.H. Tyson (Northamptonshire), T.G. Evans (Kent), G.P.S. Delisle (Middlesex), D. Bennett (Middlesex), A.C. Walton (Middlesex), S. Singh (Cambridge University), W.J. Edrich (Middlesex), A.E. Moss (Middlesex), E. Smith (Derbyshire), D.V.P. Wright (Kent), C.C.P. Williams (Oxford University). Yorkshire made 238 for 9 and 237 for 5 both declared, with the MCC scoring 113 and 174. Yorkshire won by 188 runs at 3.03 p.m. on the third day.

The MCC *v*. Yorkshire in 1957. From left to right: B. Taylor (Essex), R.A. Gale (Middlesex), E.R. Dexter (Sussex), J.J. Warr (Middlesex), F.H. Tyson (Northamptonshire), W.J. Edrich (Middlesex), T.E. Bailey (Essex), D.J. Insole (Essex), G. Goonesena (Cambridge University), A.C. Walton (Middlesex), D.J. Shepherd (Glamorgan). Yorkshire won by eight wickets at 3.25 p.m. on the third day, with scores of 267 and 78 for 2. The MCC made 173 and 170.

Colin Ingleby-Mackenzie of Hampshire and Mike Smith of Warwickshire walking out to bat for the MCC *v*. Yorkshire in 1958. The pair shared a fourth-wicket partnership of 32 runs; Mike Smith scored 72 and Colin Ingleby-Mackenzie 15.

Trevor Bailey of Essex and Colin Ingleby-Mackenzie of Hampshire appearing during the MCC's fixture against Yorkshire in 1959. Trevor Bailey made 37 not out and Colin Ingleby-Mackenzie 50 and between them contributed 78 for the fifth wicket.

Barry Knight of Essex and Ken Barrington of Surrey about to bat for the MCC against Yorkshire in 1962. The pair added 48 for the sixth wicket in the second innings. Ken Barrington scored 107 and Barry Knight 23.

The North XI which met the South XI in 1947. From left to right: W. Place (Lancashire), R. Pollard (Lancashire), K. Cranston (Lancashire), D.V. Brennan (Yorkshire), H.J. Butler (Nottinghamshire), J. Hardstaff (Nottinghamshire), N.W.D. Yardley (Yorkshire), L. Hutton (Yorkshire), J.H. Wardle (Yorkshire), C. Washbrook (Lancashire), D. Brookes (Northamptonshire). Cyril Washbrook and Norman Yardley both contributed centuries to the North's innings, with 129 and 126 respectively.

Ken Cranston of Lancashire and Norman Yardley of Yorkshire appearing in the North *v.* South fixture in 1947. The pair added 7 for the sixth wicket.

Len Hutton of Yorkshire and Cyril Washbrook of Lancashire walking out to bat for the North against the South in the same match. The pair added 37 for the first wicket. Len Hutton made 17 and Cyril Washbrook 129.

The South XI in the 1947 match with the North. From left to right: J.A. Young (Middlesex), L.B. Fishlock (Surrey), W.W. Wooller (Glamorgan), R.E.S. Wyatt (Worcestershire), F.R. Brown (Northamptonshire), A.V. Bedser (Surrey), A.W.H. Mallett (Oxford University), T.G. Evans (Kent), R. Howorth (Worcestershire), M.P. Donnelly (Oxford University), D.R. Wilcox (Essex). The South took the first innings by 177 runs but the match was drawn on the third day. Centuries were recorded for the South XI by Laurie Fishlock (120), Martin Donnelly (113) and Freddie Brown (104 not out).

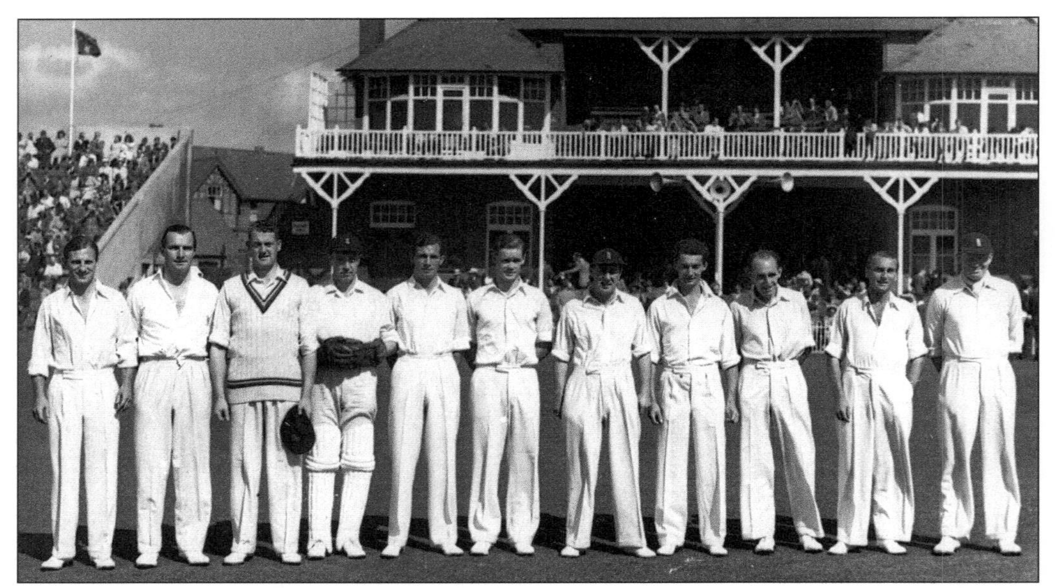

The North XI in 1949. From left to right: L. Hutton (Yorkshire), K. Cranston (Lancashire), C. Gladwin (Derbyshire), G.O. Dawkes (Derbyshire), V. Broderick (Northamptonshire), D.B. Close (Yorkshire), N.W.D. Yardley (Yorkshire), R.T. Simpson (Nottinghamshire), E.I. Lester (Yorkshire), J. Hardstaff (Nottinghamshire), F.R. Brown (Northamptonshire). North XI won on first innings by 35 runs and the match was drawn at 6.00 p.m. on the third day. Norman Yardley made 159 and Len Hutton 101 for the North.

Reg Simpson of Nottinghamshire and Len Hutton of Yorkshire during the North *v.* South fixture in 1949. The pair added 110 for the first wicket, with Len Hutton scoring 54 and Reg Simpson 78.

The South side for the same match. From left to right: T.W. Graveney (Gloucestershire), A.J. Watkins (Glamorgan), R.O. Jenkins (Worcestershire), L.B. Fishlock (Surrey), J.A. Young (Middlesex), R.E.S. Wyatt (Worcestershire), T.N. Pearce (Essex), A.I. McIntyre (Surrey), D.J. Insole (Essex), A.V. Bedser (Surrey), R. Smith (Essex). Hundreds recorded for the South XI were Bob Wyatt (125), Laurie Fishlock (112) and Ray Smith (112).

Bob Wyatt of Warwickshire and Laurie Fishlock of Surrey about to bat for the South in 1949. They both made centuries (125 and 112 respectively) and contributed 189 runs for the first wicket.

The North XI in 1950. From left to right: D. Kenyon (Worcestershire), G. Lester (Leicestershire), L. Hutton (Yorkshire), J.E. Walsh (Leicestershire), C. Gladwin (Derbyshire), M. Hilton (Lancashire), R.T. Simpson (Nottinghamshire), D.V. Brennan (Yorkshire), N.W.D. Yardley (Yorkshire), L.G. Berry (Leicestershire), E.I. Lester (Yorkshire).

Bill Edrich of Middlesex and Michael Walford of Somerset about to bat for the South in 1950. The pair added 22 for the second wicket, with Bill Edrich scoring 13 and Michael Walford 34.

The South XI in 1950. From left to right: T.W. Graveney (Gloucestershire), W.E. Jones (Glamorgan), T.P.B. Smith (Essex), W.J. Edrich (Middlesex), D.J. Insole (Essex), S.C. Griffith (Sussex), T.E. Bailey (Essex), L.B. Fishlock (Surrey), J.A. Young (Middlesex), R. Smith (Essex). The South won by three wickets at 5.58 p.m. on the third day.

An XI from the rest of the counties which played the champions Surrey in 1957. From left to right: F.H. Tyson (Northamptonshire), P.W. Richardson (Worcestershire), D.C.S. Compton (Middlesex), D.W. Richardson (Worcestershire), T.W. Graveney (Gloucestershire), T.E. Bailey (Essex), F.S. Trueman (Yorkshire), T.G. Evans (Kent), J.H. Wardle (Yorkshire), R.E. Marshall (Hampshire), G.E. Tribe (Northamptonshire). Surrey won by six wickets at 5.25 p.m. on the third day.

Roy Marshall of Hampshire and Peter Richardson of Worcestershire walking out to bat for The Rest *v*. Surrey in 1957. The pair shared a first-wicket partnership of 85; Peter Richardson scored 32 and Roy Marshall 55.

Roger Prideaux of Northamptonshire and Ken Barrington of Surrey walking out to bat at Scarborough during a Festival match in 1962.

Six

The Personalities

The Gilligan brothers seen at the North Marine Road ground in 1925. Arthur (left) played for Sussex and Frank for Essex.

Jim Smith of Middlesex leaves the Pavilion at North Marine Road on his way to the wicket during a Festival match at Scarborough in 1928.

K.S. Duleepsinhji of Sussex at the North Marine Road ground in 1928.

Middlesex's Jack Durston signs autographs for the local youngsters at the North Marine Road ground during the Scarborough Festival of 1928.

Yorkshire's Wilfred Rhodes pictured in his Yorkshire CCC blazer and cap within the players' enclosure of the pavilion during the 1930 Festival.

Herbert Sutcliffe of Yorkshire and England pictured in the field at North Marine Road during the Cricket Festival in 1931.

Jack Hobbs of Surrey and England in the players' enclosure of the pavilion balcony at North Marine Road at the 1932 Festival.

Eddie Paynter of Lancashire and England leaves the Pavilion at North Marine Road on his way to the wicket during a Festival match at Scarborough in 1933.

Bob Wyatt of Warwickshire and Wally Hammond of Gloucestershire walking out to bat at Scarborough during a Festival match in 1933.

Above left: K.S. Duleepsinhji of Sussex and Andy Sandham of Surrey preparing to bat in 1933. *Above right:* Jack Hobbs of Surrey and K.S. Duleepsinhji of Sussex coming onto the field, also in 1933. *Below left:* K.S. Duleepsinhji of Sussex and Wilfred Rhodes of Yorkshire take the field at Scarborough during a Festival match in 1933. *Below right*: Henry Enthoven of Middlesex and Alexander Kennedy of Hampshire take the field during the Cricket Festival of 1934.

Arthur Wood (wicketkeeper) and Tom Smailes, both of Yorkshire, pose for the photographers as they take the field at North Marine Road during the Festival in 1934.

Hedley Verity of Yorkshire and Bill Voce of Nottinghamshire walking out to bat at Scarborough during a Festival match in 1934.

Above left: Herbert Sutcliffe of Yorkshire and Walter Keeton of Nottinghamshire walking out to bat at Scarborough during a Festival match in 1934. *Above right:* Henry Enthoven of Middlesex and Bob Wyatt of Warwickshire at the 1934 Festival. *Below left:* Bob Wyatt of Warwickshire and William Fairservice of Kent walking out to bat at the 1935 Festival. *Below right:* Freddie Brown of Northamptonshire and Bob Wyatt of Warwickshire in 1935.

Arthur Mitchell of Yorkshire leaves the Pavilion on his way to the wicket during a Festival match in 1936.

From left to right: Bill Bowes of Yorkshire, Errol Holmes of Surrey and a playing member of the Indian touring team view the cricket at the 1936 Festival.

Above left: Maurice Leyland of Yorkshire and Joe Hardstaff of Nottinghamshire walking out to bat in 1936. *Above right:* John Richardson and Brian Sellers, both of Yorkshire, walking out to bat in 1937. *Below left:* Bob Wyatt of Warwickshire and Maurice Leyland of Yorkshire during a Festival match in 1937. *Below right:* Hedley Verity of Yorkshire and Bob Wyatt of Warwickshire, also seen in 1937.

Above left: Len Hutton of Yorkshire and Bob Wyatt of Warwickshire during a Festival match in 1937. *Above right:* Middlesex and England's Patsy Hendren leaves the Pavilion at North Marine Road on his way to the wicket during a Festival match in 1937. *Below left:* Sussex and England's Billy Griffith at the North Marine Road ground in 1938. *Below right:* Maurice Leyland of Yorkshire and England at the Festival in 1938.

Above left: Gubby Allen of Middlesex and Billy Griffith of Sussex walking out to bat in 1938. *Above right*: Paul Gibb of Essex leaving the field after being dismissed in 1938. *Below left*: Bill Edrich of Middlesex and Basil Allen of Cambridge University and Gloucestershire in 1938. *Below right:* Arthur Mitchell and Len Hutton, both of Yorkshire, walking out to bat in 1947.

Above left: Freddie Brown of Northamptonshire and John Dewes of Middlesex walking onto the pitch in 1948. *Above right:* Alec Bedser of Surrey and Tom Pritchard of Warwickshire in 1948. *Below left:* 'Gami' Goonasena of Cambridge University, Ceylon, Nottinghamshire and New South Wales pictured during the Cricket Festival in 1951. *Below right:* Doug Insole of Cambridge University, Essex and England in 1951.

The Lancashire and Yorkshire combined 'Red and White Rose' ladies team which played a Rest of England ladies team at the Festival in 1949.

The Rest of England ladies XI in 1949.

John Warr of Cambridge University, Middlesex and England pictured at North Marine Road in 1951.

'The twins' Eric and Alec Bedser of Surrey at Scarborough in 1952.

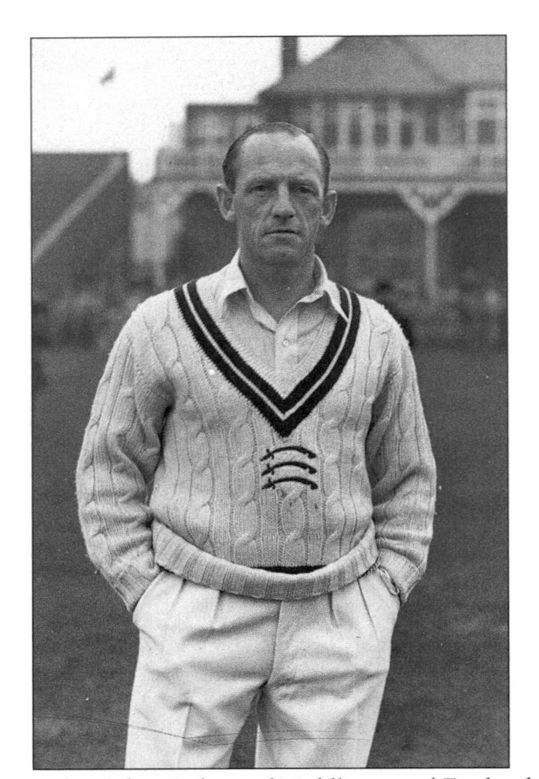

Left: Walter Robins of Middlesex and England at the 1952 Festival.
Right: Robin Marlar of Cambridge University, Sussex and England in 1953.

Len Hutton of Yorkshire and England with Douglas Jardine of Surrey and England at the Festival in 1958.

Johnny Wardle of Yorkshire and England pictured at Scarborough in 1957.

Frank Tyson of Northamptonshire and John Warr of Middlesex walking out to bat at Scarborough during a Festival match in 1962.

Geoffrey Boycott and Ken Taylor, both of Yorkshire, walk out to the wicket at the 1963 Festival.

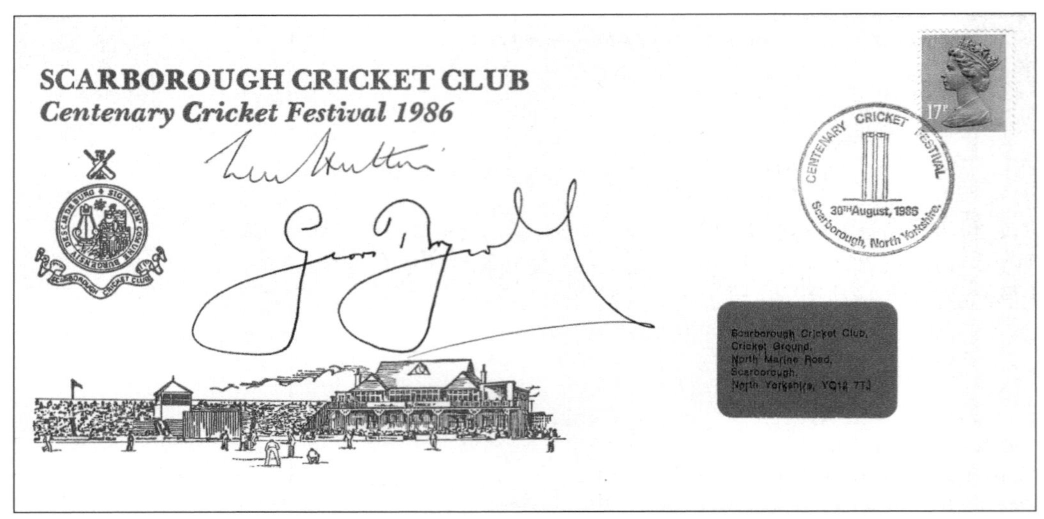

A First Day Cover to celebrate the Centenary Cricket Festival in 1986. It was posted on 30 August 1986 and is signed by Len Hutton and Geoffrey Boycott of Yorkshire.

Seven

North Marine Road

Scarborough Cricket Club leased the North Marine Road ground from 1863 for £15 a year, until they purchased it outright in 1878. Cricket has been played in Scarborough since 1849 when the town's cricket club was founded. The club's first matches were staged at Castle Hill (also known as the Queen's Cricket Ground, which has long since been built on) elsewhere in the town. Yorkshire CCC staged matches at Castle Hill between 1874 and 1877 and have visited the North Yorkshire seaside resort on the coast ever since 1874 for matches each season, usually in July or September. This picture of the ground was taken in 1905 during a Festival match and shows Wilfred Rhodes of Yorkshire bowling to the Australian captain Warwick Armstrong.

The Johnny Walker Scoreboard is situated on the beach front to enable holidaymakers on the beach to keep up to date with the score from the Test match, and is seen here in 1926.

The first Festival of matches was staged in 1876 and the first first-class match staged by Yorkshire at North Marine Road was against I'Zingari in 1878. The first first-class Cricket Festival was staged in 1886 when the teams were Rangers CC, Yorkshire CCC, Marylebone CC and Scarborough CC. This picture illustrates the view from the bandstand near the Presidents' Tent, looking towards the pavilion during a Festival match in 1955.

The original pavilion erected in 1874 was replaced at a cost of £2,150 in 1895. The new building still stands today in the north-west corner of the ground. Before the first County Championship match on the ground, staged by Yorkshire when their opponents were Leicestershire in 1896, the pavilion clock was presented as a gift to the Scarborough Cricket Club by Mr & Mrs J. Compton-Rickett and Mr J.H. Morton. The Scarborough CC has remained one of the best organized in the country for many years, thanks in the main to the efforts of Mr Robert Barker, the Secretary at the time of its formation, and its distinguished presidents, including the Rt Hon. Lord Hawke, the Earl of Londesborough and Mr H.D.G. Leveson-Gower. This picture shows a view of the ground in 1957 during a Festival match.

In 1902, thanks to funds generated from a successful Cricket Festival, a new seating enclosure was erected; it was extended in the following year and again in 1907. In 1903 a Press Box/Scorers' Room was constructed at a cost of £250. It was not until after the First World War that further development took place at the ground, when a new concrete stand was built in the north-east corner in 1926. This aerial picture shows the ground full to the brim during a Festival match in 1962.

The West Stand was built in 1956 and is the most recent addition to the ground. This aerial view of the ground, taken in 1986, looking out to sea, shows clearly the West Stand, sited to the left of the marquees and President's Enclosure.

View of the Pavilion at the Scarborough Cricket Festival in 1992.